*Squit, Wit
and...
Shifty Tales*

*Dedicated to my Norfolk family of friends,
bearing in mind that a true friend is someone
who knows you well - and still likes you.*

Keith Skipper

*An optimist laughs to forget —
A pessimist forgets to laugh.*

Squit, Wit and... Shifty Tales

Keith Skipper

Toftwood, Dereham, Norfolk

Published by:
NOSTALGIA PUBLICATIONS
(Terry Davy)
7 Elm Park, Toftwood,
Dereham, Norfolk NR19 1NB

First Impression October 1995
Reprinted on publication
Reprinted January 1996

© Nostalgia Publications 1995

ISBN 0 947630 12 0

All rights reserved. No part of this publication may be reproduced, stored in a retrieval system, or transmitted in any form or by any means, electronic, mechanical, photocopying, recording, or otherwise, without prior permission of the publisher

Design and Typesetting:
NOSTALGIA PUBLICATIONS

Printed by:
COLOURPRINT
Fakenham, Norfolk

Contents

Acknowledgements 6
Foreword by Hadrian Mule (aged 87¾) 8
Thass a Larf! 11
Don't Panic! 18
All Preachers 23
Aunt Agatha 28
Right Replies 31
Screen Gems 34
Bard to Worse 40
The Name Game 43
What They Mean 50
Diss Delights 54
Write Away! 56
Bus Pass 61
John Willy 63
Trendy List 66
Dora's Dumplins 67
Hello, my Bewty! 69
The Old Days 73
You Don't Say! 77
The Fame Game 80
Dippy's Tune 84
Dodman Lane 88
Rural Rides 92

Acknowledgements

OBSERVANT readers will notice my taking liberties with photographs of people and places they could well recognise. This is deliberate in the name of whimsy - so please don't write, ring or report me to a higher authority.

The whole pictorial exercise featuring a series of "Norfolk firsts" has been conducted in keeping with the light-hearted flavour of the book, and I hope my puckish intentions give no offence.

For their cheerful support on the illustration front I thank: Jim Baldwin and other members of Fakenham Local History Society, Ron Shaw and his friends in Litcham Historical Society, Erica and Michael Smith of Honingham, Clifford Temple, Brian Hedge, Albert Peachment of Sparham and Eastern Counties Newspapers.

A special salute to BBC Radio Norfolk Dinnertime devotees whose limericks, letters and local laughs were tucked away for a rainy day, and all other correspondents who have eagerly provided me with humorous material over the years.

Warmest thanks to Terry Davy, at Nostalgia Publications, for showing faith in a project that might have unnerved a lesser mortal.

My customary bouquet for my wife, Diane, who has again transferred my raw material to a word processor. I may be ready to return the compliment by the time she writes her memoirs.

I am privileged to have Norfolk sage Hadrian Mule (aged 87¾) provide a witty and wholesome foreword. He even had his "likeness" taken for the first time in over 50 years to go with his golden words. Perhaps we can yet persuade him to write his life story, thus throwing more valuable light on the progress of the squit wagon in Norfolk this century.

Finally, to all who glory in our county and its special ways, my sincere gratitude for keeping the wagon rolling. A few miles to go yet, ole bewties!

Keith Skipper
Cromer 1995.

norfolk firsts

No. 1

Norfolk's first skiffle group, Captain Flint and The Stonepickers, emerged from a quarry near Litcham to be voted "Most Promising Newcomers" after an appearance on "Opportunity Rocks". But it was the introduction of the famous giant washboard that turned their 1884 tour of Stiffkey into a memorable success. Line-up (left to right): Barney Ribble (vocals), Captain Amos Flint (lute, rake and lead guitar) and Lennie Dunnegan (lyrics and giant washboard)

Foreword

by Hadrian Mule (aged 87¾)

I HEV seen a rare lot o' changes in Norfolk over the years - and I hev opposed every bloomin' one on' em!

Wuh, thass no good hevin' a surname like Mule wi'owt showin' a stubborn streak now an' agin. Reckon I'll stick ter that for rest o' my days in the best place on earth.

People keep on askin' me ter write my life story, but I arnt one fer pushin' meself forrard. I dint hev a lot of book-larnin', nor go ter one o' them posh schools up on a hill, so yew'll hatter teark me as yew find me.

Matter o' fact that took a fair bit o' arm-twistin' ter git me ter write this here, tho' I reckon two pints o' mild an' half-ounce o' best baccy is better 'an what sum on' em git fer a few hundred words.

When Mr Skipper ask me ter do this little job I thowt thass cors he coont git no-one else. But he dew insist he wanted "a true son of the soil who can sing Norfolk's praises in the right key". Dunno bowt all that, speshally as I wuz hulled out o' the local church choir in 1919 for reasons I dunt watter go into right here. Still, I did know what I wuz up tew on

Hadrian Mule (aged 87¾)

the land…sometimes my ankles when that poured o' rain. (He did say less hev a bit o' squit now an' agin.)

Yis, we do hev a sense o' humour in Norfolk, no matters what them newcomers and visitors say, and a book like this kin only dew our reputations a lot o' good. (Praps I orter asked fer three pints o' mild).

I heard an' saw lotter funny things when I worked on the farm, but there wuz a lot more on'us in them days. Yew had ter expect a bit o' squit now an' agin wi' yer grub under the hidge, an' there wuz allus chance o' findin' a toad or suffin' bigger in yar Oxo tin! Mind yew, that wunt allus cold tea "Shutknife" Parker wuz a'slurpin' - but no-one let on.

We called him "Shutknife" cors he never went nowhere wi'owt it. Blarst, he even used ter sit there runnin' his finger up an' down the blade in chapel, an' I know he nearly put it in the collection plearte five times.

Jist abowt all on' em had nicknames in our willage, and yew kin soon work out why. "Trotty" Hawes never walked nowhere. "Peg" Makin lorst his left leg in the First War. "Titch" Harmer wuz miles bigger'n ennyone else. "Smiler" Large wuz the most miserable beggar yew could ever meet; and "Splasher" Clayton had an accident when he wuz in the infants at school.

Dew yew know, everythin' seemed ter hev a reason ahind it, an' yew could keep up wi' things when they dint go ser quick. Now that all hoss past fit ter bust, so that'll dew yew good ter slow down an' enjoy "Squit, Wit and… Shifty Tales".

There's one good ole sayin' yew wunt find in here, so I'll pass that on afore I forgit… "If yar parents dint hev no children, chances are yew wunt neither!".

Fare y'well, tergether - an' keep that squit cart rollin'!

Hadrian Mule

(aged 87¾, and proud onnit)

Norfolk Firsts

No. 2

Norfolk's first professional magician, Jabez Daniels, was a star attraction at harvest suppers in the Swaffham area at the turn of the century. His favourite trick was to make a rabbit disappear completely after covering it with a sack. Audiences never knew he had a ferret in his pocket. Jabez always ended his act with the line: "I'm glad yew dint disapeer afore I finished!" He retired in 1919 after failing to turn a horse and cart into a five-acre field.

Thass a Larf!

ANY attempt to delve into the mysteries and delights of Norfolk humour must start with general agreement on two counts - Norfolk stories, especially those liberally laced with dialect, were designed to be told rather than be read, and quite a few were inspired by a close-knit agricultural world long gone.

I have resisted the temptation to simply compile a selection of "local yarns", accepting in the first place that too many of them would have done the rounds elsewhere before being given a Norfolk coat of paint.

My mission rather is to look for reasons why our humour is so special, why it is different, and to dig up some of the roots from whence it springs.

Rural wit and humour, generally called "squit" in these parts, comes to a large extent from the days when country folk had to provide their own fun or go without. They couldn't mull over the previous evening's television offerings, or titter at the excesses of the tabloid newspapers, so they shared little incidents from real life instead as another day unfolded on the village stage.

Rough and ready humour prevailed, often edged with what lesser mortals construed as spite or even cruelty. Repetition and embellishment added to the laughs, especially when the target for risible treatment came into view. Nicknames often resulted from escapades that soon became common knowledge.

> *Old William was having a serious talk with his son, who was planning to get married.*
> *"Yew want ter be careful where yew live, boy. Yew want ter meark sure the neighbours are poor dew yew'll find they'll allus be buying things yew carnt afford."*

Which farmworker put hurdles in the river to turn back the water? (They called him Canute). Who told Charlie his ladder wasn't long enough, and so sawed off a few rungs from the bottom and tied them to the top? (They called him inventive). Why did the verger insist on calling it "Holy Commotion" and annoying all the ladies? (They called him long words he didn't understand).

Country writer Clarence Henry Warren said about half-a-century ago: "It is one of the most attractive features of country humour that it never quite loses its freshness. It may be passed on from generation to generation, but it remains a coin whose mintage is never dulled with use. The same may be said of country expressions which are not necessarily humorous at all - metaphors and likenesses and odd phrases which, once coined, have never gone out of currency."

He recalled a couple of his countryman father's sayings: "It doesn't take long to do a five minute job!". And to anybody out and about unusually early in the morning, "You must have got up before you went anywhere!".

> *Four and twenty honeycarts running through the dark,*
> *With their crews of honeymen up before the lark;*
> *They're coming for your buckets, be their contents low or high;*
> *So watch the flap, my lady, while the honeycarts go by.*
>
> Nick Walmsley

Old Mr Warren might have added how often it picks a wet day to rain, or how it gets late earlier when the clocks go back.

Of course, the real beauty of country humour rests in the way the underdog bites back, the downtrodden gets up out of the nettles, the simpleton rounds on the cleverdick, the blunt object of ridicule suddenly finds a bright pin to burst the balloon of pomposity.

My favourite in this category concerns a Norfolk farmer in a jovial mood after a good harvest. He thought he'd have a bit of fun with Old Ben, who was supposed to be a few sticks short of a bundle.

"Now, Ben, take a wheelbarrow and a four-tined fork and empty the water out of the hoss-pond so it can fill up again with fresh rainwater".

Old Ben duly wandered off to collect the wheelbarrow and the fork from the other side of the farm. The farmer stood smirking as he passed. Then Old Ben turned around…

"Now, marster, afore I git on a' dewin' that there pond, wot dew yew want me ter dew wi' the water - spreed it or leave it in piles?"

Just when you think you're calling the tune…!

If Norfolk people can be rather rough on each other when the need arises, these antics pale into nothing alongside treatment meted out to less-than-gracious "furriners". Devastation is the name of the game - and it has been going on ever since the first invasion brought with it the assumption that these rustics are here for the taking.

George was showing an American tourist round the village. "Thass our chatch. Took nigh on twenty year ter bild, centuries ago."

"Gee, I guess back in Texas we could build one in five…".

"Thass our new school. Only took nine months ter bild that…".

"Gee, I guess back home we could put up a school in six months…".

They turned a corner where stood the village hall. "Say, buddy, what's that building?"

"What, over there? Dunno, ole partner - that wunt there when I cum ter work this mornin'…"

Tests also come on foreign soil, as many a Norfolk soldier can testify, but life must have been particularly fraught for girls who went into service a long way away from home. One Norfolk mawther went up to London to work in a big house where there were many other servants who laughed at her for being a "country cousin".

One day she came back from shopping and rang the doorbell for admittance. The footman let her in and remarked: "Well, here's our little country cousin back, safe and sound."

She gave him an old-fashioned Norfolk look and said: "There now, ent Lunnun a rare wunderful plearce…all yew ha' got ter dew is push a button an' out pop a fewl!".

Some stories refuse to drop into any pigeon-hole, and it's nigh impossible to suggest reasons why they are funny. I am still trying to work out why this one makes me chuckle…

A Norfolk rector was visited by an agitated old lady parishioner rather early in the morning.

"I'm wholly sorry ter trubbel yew this time o' the mornin' Rector, but I thowt praps yew could intarpret a dream I hed larst night. I dremp I saw my ole man - yew remember my Harbert, dunt yer? Well, he cum an' stand by my bedside, an' he dew look bewtiful! He got a crown on his skull, a harp in his hand an' he's a'wearin' a long, white robe. An', oh, he dew look bewtiful…"

She looked at the Rector pleadingly.

"Dew yew think that mean rain?"

> "I hear you have a new baby sister" the village shopkeeper said to young Billy. "What's her name?"
> "Dunno" replied Billy, "She carnt talk yit."

Perhaps the most elusive quality in Norfolk humour to commit to print is a stunning use of understatement. The best example I have encountered came from Dick Bagnall-Oakeley, naturalist, teacher and dialect expert.

He recalled a scene from the notorious winter of 1963 when he was making a film on the changes of habit imposed upon seabirds by prolonged exposure to hunger and severe cold. He chose a spot on the coast near Salthouse as the ideal view for a long background shot on which the credits for his film could be superimposed. He arrived a little early on a bitter February evening with the temperature reading eight degrees of frost, and he stood in the lee of a small cliff for the sun to sink to the right angle.

"One other person went down to the cold, desolate stretch of coastline that evening. He was an old beachcomber, raggedly but warmly dressed, wheeling his bicycle with him, on the off-chance that a plank might be there among the driftwood washed up by the freezing tide.

"For about 20 minutes I stood in such shelter as the cliff provided, but the sun had still not descended to the angle I wanted before the beachcomber had completed his tour and started to return.

"He passed me, still standing in eight degrees of frost, immobile in the same position as I had been in when he passed before. This time he spoke as he passed, and in the one word he uttered I heard all the plain speech, the avoidance of the play of 'polite' conversation, the laconic brevity and the shrewd humour that I have come to know and love in Norfolk people.

"Not a shabby, anonymous beachcomber, he summed himself up in an expression echoing all the ironic humour and the unanswerable understatement of a true Norfolk character.

"Sweatin'?"

Not far behind in the Norfolk understatement stakes comes this delightful runner, also from the Dick Bagnall-Oakeley stable.

Again the setting is that harsh winter of 1963. Dick was driving home in the evening after giving a talk in Cambridge.

"Driving conditions were the most atrocious I have ever known. Ruts had been ploughed by traffic in the deep snow on the road, and the snow had frozen. Gingerly I picked my way across slippery, iron-hard bars, cracks, ruts, channels and potholes.

"Going through Brandon I heard the snorting and gasping of a sports car revving up in the below-freezing temperature. Soon the car came out behind me from an inn yard, overtook me and sped off up the frozen road to Swaffham. Like the tortoise following the hare, my car continued to grind painfully through the packed snow. There was no other traffic on the road.

> *Teacher said to Charlie's class, "Will all those who think they might be stupid stand up."*
> *For a moment no-one stirred. Then Charlie got to his feet.*
> *"Charlie" said the teacher, "Do you think you are stupid?"*
> *"Nut really, miss" he replied. "I just dint like to see yew standin' there by yourself!"*

"What happened next? You've guessed it. Some way further up the Brandon-Swaffham road, in the heart of the inhospitable Breckland, in the most cruel time of the year, I saw two red lights. As I inched my car nearer, I eventually realised in the darkness that not only were they the tail lights of a sports car, not only were they off the road - but the driver had hit one of the many iron-hard mounds on the uneven road at high speed, slewed off the road and turned the car completely upside down in the ditch. There he hung, suspended upside down in his seat by a safety belt.

"I had travelled the road many times before, but I had never previously noticed a small cottage among the trees at that particular stretch. Now, however, out of it, with his shoulders bent against the wind and his lamp flickering, shuffled an old man. His comment on the situation stamped him immediately as a Norfolk man:

"What, are yer in a little bit o' a muddle?"

This Norfolk penchant for turning mountains into molehills is underlined by two yarns ready for circulation after the tremor that rocked parts of the county in 1931.

A Norfolk labourer was asked by a local press reporter if he had felt it. "Blarst, no, cors I dint…I sleep at the back o' the house!"

Then an old lady told of her experiences to anyone who cared to listen. "Oh, that wuz terrible, that wuz. The ole house started ter rock an' shearke, and th'ole bed along with it. My ole man, he got up an' looked owter the winder, an' I holler, 'John' I say, 'I berleeve thass th'inder the wald woss come!' 'Yis, Maria' he say, 'I berleeve that hev…NO! Howld yew hard. Thass orryte…them shallots is still there!'"

> *Old Ted was busy measuring up the front of his cottage with a foot rule.*
> *"What are yew dewin'?" asked Sam.*
> *"Well, bor" said Ted, "I're got this form ter fill in. I're got ter put how old I am, when and where I wuz born, my present address an' the length o' my residence."*

Understatement's natural companions are caution and economy. Sadly, they have been mistaken all too often for coldness and suspicion. Many newcomers and visitors fail to appreciate the subtlety of Norfolk humour because they have been fed a diet of slick one-liners and stereotyped images of country bumpkins chewing straw, manning drawbridges and sounding like a cross between Walter Gabriel and Adge Cutler.

Perhaps the remarkable discovery that Norfolk standard-bearers are not graduates of Mummerzet House, a big building in London where drama students can enrol for a course in country dialects, puts strangers at such a disadvantage they cast aside any charitable feelings.

Norfolk's geographical isolation has long been a source of both grudging envy and mild mockery. "On the road to nowhere" and "Bandit country" are the sort of labels the county has been stuck with. Well-meaning missionaries, while extolling Norfolk's virtues, have been quick to offer reasons for the nervous tendency.

When H. V. Morton went "In Search of England" in the 1920s, he was moved to declare: "Norfolk is the most suspicious county in England. In

Devon and Somerset men hit you on the back cordially; in Norfolk they look as though they would like to hit you over the head - till they size you up.

"You see, for centuries the North folk of East Anglia were accustomed to meet stray Vikings on lonely roads who had just waded ashore from a long boat.

"Good mornin', bor" said the Viking. "Which is the way to the church?"

"What dew yew want ter know for?" was the Norfolk retort.

"Well, we thought about setting fire to it!"

"You will gather that Norfolk's suspicion of strangers, which is an ancient complex bitten into the East Anglian through centuries of bitter experience, is well grounded, and should never annoy the traveller."

Well, some visitors still refuse to make allowances for aversion to Vikings - even Vikings without pyrotechnic inclinations - and the resultant coolness remains at the heart of the best Norfolk humour. (Judge for yourself when you reach the chapter "Right Replies").

Perhaps the style of the combatants has changed from downright confrontational to well-rehearsed teasing in this era of greater mobility and rapid change. Even so, the necessary edge is still there as the sly Norfolk way of "laying for" a stranger with an arrogant streak produces the proper outcome.

In the early days of motoring, when a lot of Norfolk roads really did lead to nowhere, a "furriner" came upon a ford at the bottom of a rutted lane. He said rather haughtily to a local standing on the footbridge: "My good man, do you think it is safe to drive through here?"

"Why yis" said the local. "I reckun yew kin drive in orryte."

The motorist drove in, only to find himself in midstream with water halfway up the bonnet.

"What the devil do you mean?" he shouted angrily." You told me this was fit for motors. You must be a complete idiot!"

"Well" said the native, "I dunt know noffin bowt motor cars, but that dunt come no more 'n harfway up our marster's ducks."

Then, having struck a bargain with the crestfallen motorist, he trudged off to fetch a horse and rope. As he went he muttered to himself with a grin: "That wuz right what I tell him bowt drivin' in. But I dint say noffin bowt drivin' owt agin."

> *A Norfolk man under the weather visited his doctor about three miles away. The doctor examined him.*
> *"Well, have you passed anything this morning?"*
> *The man thought for a moment, brightened and replied: "Oh yis, doctor ... two loads o' straw, five bikes an' a steamroller!"*

Norfolk Firsts

No. 3

Norfolk's first sponsored snow-clearing team got together at Barnham Broom in the summer of 1880 to work out a strategy for the great blizzard expected in the first months of 1881. Long-range forecasters counted berries on hedgerows and pointed to strange cloud formations over Seething as indications of bad weather to come. Blizzard conditions in January 1881 prevented the pioneering snow clearers from leaving their homes.

Don't Panic!

ONE of the most fertile acres for amusing yarns is that marched over by the Home Guard with their broomsticks, pitchforks, Boer War rifles and dedication.

Let me underline immediately how modesty lies behind all the humour and self-effacement, and it has been repeated countless times that if there had been an invasion this Dad's Army would have conducted themselves with the greatest credit and bravery.

The Local Defence Volunteers (Look, Duck and Vanish!) banded together in May, 1940. Just over two months later Winston Churchill sent out a new message of responsibility and hope when he changed the name to the Home Guard...

"This is a war of the unknown warriors. The whole of the warring nations are engaged, not only soldiers but the entire population, men, women and children. The fronts are everywhere. The trenches are dug in the towns and streets. Every village is fortified. Every road is barred. The front lines run through the factories. The workmen are soldiers with different weapons - but the same courage".

A rallying call answered enthusiastically. By "stand down", in 1944, the Home Guard had acquired a formidable array of weaponry and was trained to professional standards. But when it all started equipment was on the flimsy side, even if the spirit was strong and willing.

Bob Atkin, of Gorleston, recalled an incident from the dark days after Dunkirk when an invasion was fully expected. The Home Guard had to protect important public installations such as railways, power stations, gasworks and post offices.

> *Jack was strolling across the field when he saw Stan hoeing the sugar beet.*
> *"What time dew yew knock orff?"*
> *"Five o'clock".*
> *"He'yew got a watch?"*
> *"No, I hent got a watch."*
> *"So how dew yew know when thass tyme ter knock orff?"*
> *"Well, yew see there's a railway line over there. A train go parst at har' past five, so if I pack up harf an howr afore that git here, I know I'm bowt ryte."*

"My father was a postman in Yarmouth and I remember him telling me how the Post Office Home Guard had to mount a 24-hour guard on the main gate. Their weapons of defence against any intruder were a bag of pepper and a hammer!

"The idea was to throw pepper in their eyes and hit them with the hammer. I used to conjure up pictures of a German paratrooper armed to the teeth with grenades and a sub-machine gun allowing himself to be hit on the head with a hammer.

"The most amusing thing to me was that they didn't even have a decent hammer. They bought it from Woolworth's!"

Roy Chaplin, of Hellesdon, related a colourful story told by his father after he had come off duty - a story with echoes all over the country:

> *The Queen of Hearts, she med some tarts,*
> *But she forgot the lard.*
> *The Knave was sore, he'd cracked his jaw*
> *'Cos they wuz bloomin' hard.*
> *Said Queen of Hearts,*
> *"They're lovely tarts!",*
> *An' offered him some more.*
> *The Knave looked glum, "Yew med 'em, mum,*
> *An' yew can eat 'em, bor!"*
>
> Muriel Dennis (Upper Sheringham)

"The Home Guard had many 'listening and watching' posts in the Norwich area, and the post involved here was on the roof of the clubhouse at the Norwich municipal golf course, now absorbed into the University of East Anglia complex.

"At the time, Spring 1940, there was much rumour and concern about the possibility of a mass German airborne invasion on the flat lands of Norfolk and East Anglia. At about 11 o'clock on the evening in question a lone aircraft passed overhead and the usual guessing game took place as to whether it was one of 'ours' or one of 'theirs'. The general opinion of the section on duty, including my father, was that it was a German, recognised by the engine's throb.

"About 15 minutes later the duty watcher reported movement in a small copse some 150 yards away on the golf course. Immediately there was talk of a possible parachutist-saboteur dropped from the aircraft.

"A muster of four or five volunteers, armed only with broomsticks, rakes and a torch, left the clubhouse to round up the intruder or intruders in the copse. As they neared the copse the

> *A bookie with business in Rackheath*
> *Was really fed up to the back teeth*
> *When a punter came in*
> *With another big win*
> *His staff whipped around for a black wreath.*
>
> C. Chorley (Caister-on-Sea)

noise increased…and little glints of light could be seen in the moonlight. The section fanned out to surround the foe as they crept nearer on hands and knees, looking forward to a triumphant capture.

"Right, this was it! The patch of bushes within the copse was surrounded and on went the torch. Some half dozen hedgehogs engaged in a courting ritual were outlined in the beam.

"The volunteers were crestfallen but relieved. The little lights that had been seen resulted from moonlight dancing on the animals' eyes".

Another dramatic yarn came from Sheila Tooke, of Clippesby, who was ten when her great wartime adventure unfolded:

"Mother couldn't find my young brother's deep-bodied pram. She soon found out what had happened - father had borrowed it and strengthened it to take his own weight plus all his Home Guard kit.

"I was asked to push him to Reedham war memorial. Dad was in Halvergate Home Guard and they were having a mock raid on Reedham to try them out just in case the Germans should invade. As I was rather frightened by the whole business, I called on my grandmother to walk with me.

"On the road to Reedham on a pitch black night a cyclist came along and swore at us for walking a pram on the wrong side of the road. He pulled up right in front of the pram and his light shone into my dad's face - or so we thought.

"We arived at Reedham railway station bridge. 'Halt! Who goes there?' Reedham Home Guard were everywhere. Luckily they took one look at grandma and me and said 'You can pass…only two ladies with a baby in a pram.' I remember shaking and feeling terrified.

"Still, we got to the bottom of the bridge hill when suddenly the pram tipped up on end, and it took all our strength to get it on the move again. Not far to go! We delivered father to the war memorial, and the guard was almost scared out of his wits as he crawled out of the pram.

"He had won through! Only one other made it, and he swam the river. All of the rest of the lads got caught red-handed under a load of pea-sticks

---

> *They say country folk tend to exaggerate. Well, one Norfolk farmer sent his foreman to borrow a cross-cut saw ... his mangolds were so big he couldn't get them into the cart. Off went the foreman.*
>
> *"Please sar, my marster wood like ter borrer yar crorsscut. His mangles are ser big he carn't lift 'em itter the cart."*
>
> *"Well, bor," replied the neighbour, "dew yew tell yar marster I am wholly sorry but my crorsscut is stuck in one o' my tearters!"*

on my uncle's haulage lorry. What a laugh it caused at the time - but I don't mind admitting I was rather scared that night."

Stories abound of near-misses, mistaken identity, over-zealous sentries, military enthusiasm getting out of hand on rural safaris and self-important bigwigs being put in their place by earthy Norfolk humour.

> *My rich Uncle Fred suffered chronical,*
> *He wuz fed up wi' feelin' so bronikal,*
> *But his Harley Street quack*
> *Say "To cure it, don't clack."*
> *Then charged him a price astronomical.*
>
> Desne Clarke (Hemsby)

I like the tale from west Norfolk about the Home Guard lads being given a rare taste of the real thing, firing live ammunition on the nearby range. The officer in charge mingled to see how the troops were shaping up to this new challenge. He crouched down beside one lad and tried to estimate his progress through binoculars.

After a spell the officer said: "I can't see any of your bullets hitting the target, my good man."

The Norfolk boy sat up straight and responded without a trace of petulance: "Well, thass a rummun'...they're leavin' this end orryte, ole partner!"

A chap on parade with Briston Home Guard couldn't even hit the bank behind the targets when they were shooting at Matlaske. It was eventually discovered he couldn't close his left eye. They presented him with an eye patch. He smiled his thanks - and became one of the best marksmen in the detachment.

Then there was the occasion when a Home Guard sergeant and a Regular sergeant went to a funfair together. At the shooting gallery the Regular shot down three balls from the jets of water in three shots. His Home Guard friend shot down all six balls in one shot.

"Bloomin' marvellous!" exclaimed the Regular.

"Yis", agreed his Home Guard colleague. "But I think we'd better be orff. I're shot the mawther who pump the water!".

> *A smart chap from the BBC Two television documentary department was asking about Lord Nelson's connection with a certain Norfolk village, but he wasn't making much progress. He saw old Billy sipping his half in the corner of the pub and said, sarcastically: "Now, what can you tell me, pop? You remember Nelson, don't you?"*
> *Billy slowly looked up and replied: "Yis, but I still liked his father best."*

Norfolk Firsts

No. 4

Norfolk's first serve-yourself garage was at the bottom of a three mile loke off the A140 at Shimpling. The main inducement to pay a visit was the offer of a free wheel with every oil change. Proprietor Billy Bendam (seen in doorway) later opened a forecourt in Diss and a puncture-mending shop at Burston. He retired to Sloley, near North Walsham, where he recharged wireless accumulators for many years.

All Preachers...

A FEW years ago I decided to test Norfolk's ecclesiastical funny-bone. The result was a delightful selection of church and chapel chuckles I could dub "All Preachers Great And Small".

Anthony Trollope wrote: "There is, perhaps, no greater hardship at present inflicted on mankind in civilised and free countries than the necessity of listening to sermons."

By the time I was asked to sample a village chapel diet of three sermons on a Sunday, plus Tuesday Fellowship if the cricketers hadn't got a crucial fixture or the school homework hadn't piled up, preachers with a largely simple but warmingly effective style had moved into our pulpits.

Indeed, colourful characters with a memorable turn of phrase were on the march a century ago if a story from the Great Yarmouth Circuit is any yardstick.

A preacher who lived in Hickling didn't even own a bike so he used to walk to his appointments. On one occasion he was on the plan to go to Yarmouth Temple Church, and set out from Hickling by rowing to Potter Heigham bridge. He walked from there to Yarmouth, a distance of about 11 miles.

The old preacher's opening remarks to his congregation... "Well, here we are tergether. Yew hev bin used ter new milk here, but this tyme yew'll hatter put up wi' skimmed. An' thass bin swulked from thuther sider Hicklin' Broad!"

> *A Norfolk woman wasn't satisfied with the quality of milk supplied by the farmer. So she decided to send her son with two tins for it. The farmer asked why.*
> *"Please sar" says the boy, "Mum say will yew put water in one tin and milk in thuther - and she'll mix it harself".*

Colin Riches, a Methodist minister who produced two books of Bible stories in Norfolk dialect, "Dew Yew Lissen Hare" and "Orl Bewtiful An' New", has rightly drawn attention to the homely illustrations used by the old lay preachers. One used to remind his hearers every spring and summer of God's providential care - "The Lord, he knew what he wuz a' dewin', mearkin' rhubarb afore strawberries!"

Another yarn to come my way concerned a travelling Norfolk preacher in the days when open-air services were common events. He arrived at the village green where a local supporter had loaned a big, empty barrel for the preacher to stand on so he could be seen and clearly heard.

The hymns were sung lustily. The congregation listened attentively to the Bible reading. Another hymn, and then the preacher announced his text… "Lo, I am with yew, but sewn yew will see me not."

Suddenly there was a loud crack and a bang as the unfortunate preacher disappeared into the barrel. Silent reverence gave way to guffaws of laughter as those nearby tried to retrieve the trapped preacher. It was hopeless to continue with the service, so a quick "The day Thou gavest, Lord, has ended" dismissed the gathering.

> *Simple Simon, simple soul,*
> *Bought a book on birth control.*
> *Judging from his wife's condition*
> *Must have been a cheap edition!*
>
> Ralph Clay (Mundesley)

This escapade did the travelling messenger a bit of good. The tale went ahead of him from village to village. Larger crowds than usual turned up - hoping, no doubt, for a repeat performance.

Episodes tinged with embarrassment stand out in my collection. Like the formidable preacher from America who was holding forth when a mother stood to take out her crying baby.

"My dear lady" implored the preacher, "don't take your baby out. He's not bothering me at all."

"He may not be" replied the mother, "but you're bothering him!"

Cyril Jolly, Methodist stalwart and raconteur from Gressenhall, told us about Ernest Banham, of Cromer, taking an afternoon service in a village chapel and then going to tea with a lady member of the congregation.

> *Posh lady to bus driver as she hands over a ten pound note: "Oh dear, I do not seem to have a 50 pence piece for the fare."*
> *Bus driver to posh lady: "Dunt yew fret my ole bewty, in a minnit yew'll hev nineteen of 'em!"*

After the evening service he went home and discovered to his dismay that he had the lady's table napkin in his pocket. He returned it, washed and ironed, with a note of apology. The lady acknowledged the return of the napkin and said: "I knew you had it, Mr Bartram, for during the sermon I saw you take it from your pocket and blow your nose on it."

Cyril also passed on this little gem. At Wendling Chapel many years ago the preacher noticed two women in the back row talking during the singing of a hymn. He held up his hands and stopped the singing abruptly. In the silence one of the women was heard to say: "Yis, and I allus fry mine in lard".

Jack Gaskin, the Hindringham baker who extolled the virtues of the Bread of Life from the pulpit in such an endearing manner, took me to Sparham Chapel on a hot Sunday afternoon.

"A dear old friend from Norwich was preaching about Moses taking the Children of Israel through the Red Sea. Time was getting on and people were starting to nod off. At last, Grandfather Cooper called out: 'Don't you think thass about time you finished, brother?'

> *Little Miss Muffet sat on her tuffet*
> *Eating her curds and whey,*
> *Along came a farmer*
> *And said to this charmer,*
> *"Yar dumplins' look luvley terday!"*
>
> Norman Guest (Norwich)

"'I can't git 'em through!' came the loud reply. Grandfather Cooper shouted even louder: 'Well, brother, praps you'll git 'em through next time you come!'."

The Bishop of Norwich, the Rt. Rev. Peter Nott, soon got to grips with the Norfolk way of keeping matters in perspective:

"I was taking a communion service in a freezing church in west Norfolk. When it was over I walked to the back of the church. My hands were completely numb with cold and I had great difficulty grasping the mug of hot coffee the churchwarden gave me.

'My goodness, your church is cold' I said.

'Oh yis, Bishop, that is cold' said the churchwarden.'But yew should be here when we dunt hev the heatin' on.'"

> *Horry went to see the doctor with knee trouble. After a thorough examination the doctor said he thought the pain in the right knee was due to old age.*
> *"I sharnt hev that" said Horry, "Both my knees are the same age - an' the uther wun's orryte!"*

When he was Bishop of Lynn, the Rt.Rev.David Bentley, was tickled by a little incident at a confirmation at St.Peter Mancroft in Norwich.

"I was dressed, of course, in my cope and mitre and came down to join a group of Sunday school children who ended the service by singing a very charming hymn in which the whole congregation were asked to join.

"One of the little boys standing near me gave me a long look and then turned to his mother and whispered: 'What is that magician going to do now?' "

One of my favourite bishop-flavoured stories concerns the rustic golf caddy who was warned to watch his language. Cook told him straight: "Marster hev Bishop stayin' longer him an' they want yew ter caddy termorrer. Jest yew watch yar tongue, bor, an' dunt yew cum out wi' none o' them narsty wads frunter them."

> *The gal Nellie came home from the photographer's. She showed Horry the picture. "That dew mearke me look a lot older 'an what I am." "Thassorryte" says Horry, "that'll searve yew th'expense o' hevin' nuther one took learter on!"*

At the sixth his lordship sent the ball soaring out of sight and a sizeable chunk of turf with it. Repairing the latter he inquired:

"Where did the sod go?"

The caddy looked him straight in the eye. "In the bludder ditch, ole partner, and dunt fergit, thass yew what started it!"

Another sporting saga as we give thanks bishops have a divine sense of humour. A young curate was bowling to a bishop playing for the visiting cricket team. He thought he'd be kind and get him off the mark with a gentle full toss. The bishop promptly hit it out of the ground.

"Sorry, young man" smiled the bishop. "I seem to have hit you right out of your parish." This annoyed the curate. He went back to his mark, roared in and sent down a fiery bouncer which struck the bishop in the midriff.

"So sorry, m'lord" said the curate. "I seem to have hit you in the middle of your diocese."

Finally, this ecumenical extravaganza features Horry the verger in a small Norfolk parish. He had been poorly and it was arranged for him to be examined by a London specialist. On his return he said to the rector: "I am in a werry bad way, marster. I must not dig enny more greaves or toll the bells or dew noffin' what put a strearn on m'body, an' I want yew ter pray for me o'Sunday."

"Well, what exactly is wrong with you, Horace?"

"I hev got a floatin' kidney."

"Oh" smiled the rector, "If I say that prayers are asked for our dear verger Horace who has a floating kidney, then I'm afraid the congregation will laugh."

"Oh ah" mused Horry. "Oh ah. Well, congregearshun dint larf thuther Sunday when yew prayed for loose livers."

> *Ole Martha say, "Cor, thass surprisin',*
> *Am I right or simply surmisin'*
> *Tha' Billa, th'ole fule*
> *Hev started tew drule*
> *Cors thass Spring an' th'ole sap's a-risin'!"*
>
> Steve Taylor (Old Catton)

norfolk firsts

No. 5

Norfolk's first flying squad policeman was Sergeant "Swoop" Swinfield, scourge of criminals on the run in mid-Norfolk during the early years of the century. An invitation to "accompany me to the station" meant a free ride on his crossbar until he was fined ten shillings and had his cycle clips confiscated for carrying three passengers over the limit. He had apprehended the notorious James brothers on suspicion of receiving stolen parsnips. Sergeant Swinfield ended his career with Interpol (Bicycle Division) at Winfarthing.

Aunt Agatha

SIDNEY Grapes of Potter Heigham wrote the much-loved Boy John Letters to the Eastern Daily Press from 1946 until his death in 1958. Invariably they carried a little philosophical gem at the end, and many readers found it difficult to wait until they had read the letter before turning to Aunt Agatha's latest homely aphorism.

Born in 1888, the son of a carpenter and builder, Sidney Grapes enjoyed local fame for many years as a Norfolk dialect comedian before he penned the first Boy John Letter just after the war. The postscript on that occasion was clearly designed to raise morale - "Aunt Agatha, she say when the war wus on there wus peace to look forward to; now there earnt, but as she say, we shall have to keep a'doin'."

Subsequent lines of wisdom were kept shorter as news flowed in about the Boy John, Granfar, the cantankerous ould Mrs W....and the rest of the little family of Norfolk characters drawn from the heart of village life.

Aunt Agatha's sayings are still quoted freely, and not just among local dialect enthusiasts; they have a much wider appeal than that. Indeed, several of her proverbs ring out in other areas, for she simply gave them her own special Norfolk coat of paint. The pattern continues. Recently I heard: "Aunt Agatha she say - Patience is puttin' up with people you would rather put down!". And you won't find that at the end of any Boy John letter.

> *At a sale Charlie offered a bid*
> *For a gun, an' that corst him ten quid.*
> *That wuz old an' corroded,*
> *But, wust of all, loaded ...*
> *"Cor blarst me!" he say - an' that did!*
>
> Anne Valentine (Blackborough)

Here's a selection of my favourites from those she did make the most of:
- Aunt Agatha, she say - The only ordinary people in our willages are them whot think they arnt.
- Aunt Agatha, she say - Many a woman hev lorst a good sweetheart by a'marryin' on him.
- Aunt Agatha, she say - Thass no good a'puttin' yar foot down if you hent got a leg to stand on.

- Granfar, he say - Salt is whot mearke tearters tearste narsty if yer dunt put it in.
- Aunt Agatha, she say - She's a werry wise woman whot say noffin at the right time.
- Aunt Agatha, she say - All husbands are alike…only they hev diffrunt fearces so you kin tell 'em apart.
- Aunt Agatha, she say - Never hit a man when he's down - he might git up agin.
- Aunt Agatha, she say - Reality is when you leave datty dishes in the sink - and them beggars are still there when you git hoom.
- Aunt Agatha, she say - If you want ter keep friends wi' the people in yar willage, keep orff the parish cownsil.
- Aunt Agatha, she say - We are orl sent her ter help the others. Granfar say, well…whot are the others sent for?
- Aunt Agatha, she say - You carnt keep trouble from cummin, but you dunt have ter give it a chair ter sit on.
- Aunt Agatha, she say - You kin allus tell a Norfolk man - but you carnt tell him much.
- Aunt Agatha, she say - Thass good ter chearnge yer mind now an agin. That help ter keep it clean.
- Aunt Agatha, she say - The chachyards are full of people the wald couldn't do without.
- Aunt Agatha, she say - A thrippeny bit ent so good as sixpence, thow that go ter chach moor often.
- Aunt Agatha, she say - That dunt matter whot happen, there's allus someone knew that wood.
- Aunt Agatha, she say - I dunt like ter repeat gossip…but whot else kin you dew with it.
- Granfar, he say - If wimmun know so much, how cum they arsk ser menny questions?
- Aunt Agatha, she say - There's only one thing wuss than bein' talked abowt. Thass not bein' talked abowt.
- Aunt Agatha, she say - She's werry glad she wunt born afore tea wuz invented.
- Aunt Agatha, she say - You kin mearke many a false step by standin' still.
- Aunt Agatha, she say - The more you say, the less people remember.
- Aunt Agatha, she say - Women love the simple things in life - like MEN!
- P.S. Ould Mrs W., she say - Thass a pity Aunt Agatha hent got noffin better ter dew!

> *A cheeky domestic servant was told by her mistress that she had enough brass in her neck to make a copper kettle.*
> *"Yis", says the maid, "An' there's enuff worter in yar ole skull ter fill it!"*

Norfolk Firsts

No. 6

Norfolk's first cross-country mail service ran from Postwick to Brundall between 1903 and 1907. The wagon was covered for the Christmas rush of 1904 following complaints about soggy letters, crumpled parcels and circulars smelling of horse manure. Penny White, with Postwick Pat holding the reins, were both put out to grass when the Post Office invested in a bicycle for their man at Cantley.

Right Replies

NEWCOMERS and strangers have long considered themselves to be much smarter than the Norfolk yokels - only to be put firmly in their place by native wit and wisdom. He may deliver his response in a slow and deliberate manner, but the old boy over the hedge invariably leaves his inquisitor on the ropes.

Arrogance and sarcasm are met with the sharpest answers. What was good enough for the Americans during the war should suffice to see off the rising young executive leaning out of his sleek new car...

- Have you lived here all your life?
  No, not yit I hent!
- How do I get to Fakenham?
  I shunt start from here if I wuz yew!
- Where does this road go to, my good man?
  That dunt go nowhere - that stays here where thass wanted!
- Why are the church bells ringing?
  Cors sumwun's a'pullin' the rope!
- Do you have matins in your church?
  No - we hev lino ryte up ter the altar!
- Do you think the farmer could use me on the land?
  No - they've got speshul stuff fer that!
- You don't know very much, do you?
  Thass as myte be - but I ent lorst!
- Get a move on...can't you see I'm in a hurry?
  If yew're in such a hurry, why dint yew start yesterday?
- Why didn't you tell me the road was blocked, you stupid fool?
  Yew never arst me!
- Where are you going to, my good fellow?
  Ent goin' nowhere - Iym just a'cummin back!

> *Some Norfolk children were playing Mums and Dads in the lane as the parson came by. He smiled, and then saw one small disconsolate boy sitting round the corner, well away from the rest. The parson asked why he wasn't playing with the others.*
> *"But I am, sar" said the little one.*
> *"And what part would you be playing then, my child?"*
> *"Please sar, I'm the little ole bearby woss waitin' ter be born."*

- How far apart should I plant these potatoes?
  Harf in your garden - an' harf in myne!
- Your potatoes are on the small side this year…
  Ah, well, I grow 'em ter fit my mouth, nut yours!
- Does this village have many amenities to talk of?
  We're got tew dokters an' wun semetery!
- Can I trust you to keep a secret?
  Oh yis…thass them I tell it tew what carnt!
- Are you in favour of progress?
  Yis, as long as nobody change noffin'
- Excuse me, but haven't you got that wheelbarrow upside down?
  No, I hent…If I had it uther way up sum fewl wood put suffin' in it!
- Why on earth are you pulling that piece of string?
  Well, dew yew cum an' try pushin' it!
- Is that river good for fish?
  Rekon that must be - I carnt git enny ter leave it!
- I suppose you have rung the Old Year out and the New Year in?
  Yis, marster, hundreds o'tymes!
- How would you like to be up there in that aeroplane?
  Well, I sartanly wunt want ter be up there wi'owt it!
- I see they buried poor old Horace Staines yesterday…
  Well, he wuz dead!
- Have you had your eyes checked?
  No - they've allus bin blew!
- How far do you reckon I am from Norwich?
  Oh, bowt the searme distance as me!
- Are you going to old Jacob's funeral?
  No - an' I dunt rekun he'll cum ter myne!
- A return ticket? Certainly…where to?
  Wuh, back here o'corse!
- When your grandfather died, how much money did he leave?
  Blarst, orl of it - you hev tew!

> *"Cleer yew orff, yew yung beggars!" bawled Fred,*
> *When they raided his strawberry bed,*
> *"Gran's rownd at yer mother's*
> *Fer sum jampots an' covers,*
> *If she fynd yew, yew'll wish yew wuz dead!"*
>
> Moya Leighton (Norwich)

> *Barney's gut-eark put him in a fix,*
> *His medicine take two hours to mix,*
> *He say "Thass no fun,*
> *Yar elevenses at one,*
> *And havin' yar fourses at six!"*
>
> John Hammond (Beccles)

ᴎorfolk firsts

No. 7

Norfolk's first "meals on wheels" service brought hot soup and custard to elderly folk living in remote areas around Long Stratton in the winter of 1885. The "mule ticket" or "helpings on the hoof" lasted three years before badly rutted lanes made it impossible to transport any liquid food this way. Social services provided a coach and pair for Christmas deliveries in 1888.

Screen Gems

NORFOLK has long been a favourite haunt for cinema and television crews, with so many unspoilt areas and charmingly old-fashioned locations asking for visits.

North Norfolk's natural beauty, heightened at regular intervals by fresh flutters in favour of the Poppyland fashion started by Clement Scott in 1883, is constantly in demand. From the grandeur of Blickling Hall to the rustic serenity of Heydon village green, this is rich territory for the image-sellers.

"The Wicked Lady", a successful film made in 1945 and starring Margaret Lockwood and James Mason, relished the Norfolk flavour. Eight years later, "Conflict of Wings", starring John Gregson, Muriel Pavlov and Harry Fowler, featured plenty of scenes shot at Hickling, Catfield and Wells. Villagers were fighting to save a bird sanctuary from being taken over by the RAF as a rocket range. The local accents were far from convincing - a fault sadly still very much in evidence whenever Norfolk voices are supposed to be heard on a national or international stage.

"The Go-Between", adapted from L. P. Hartley's novel in 1971, had Julie Christie and Alan Bates in starring roles and a lot of location work in the county. King's Lynn played a leading part in "Revolution" in 1986, when Al Pacino and Donald Sutherland were among the big names in town. The film about the American Revolution was a flop, but the local economy collected a handy fillip.

Countless television series have enjoyed a Norfolk background - "Dad's Army" on manoeuvres in Breckland and Albert Campion driving his Lagonda around Mundford immediately catch the eye - and many other production units will be heading this way in the years to come. There are still parts of Norwich where the clip-clop of horses has an authentic ring, while we must cherish the picturesque villages unsullied by too much progress.

> *A good Norfolk man died and went to Heaven. St Peter met him and asked where he came from.*
> *"Cromer, bor".*
> *St. Peter shook his head. "Rum ole dew ... carnt see 'em mearkin' Norfolk dumplins fer one!"*

In the meantime, those most devoted to the cinema will be swift to salute the Norfolk connection in so many classics of the silver screen. Even that most distinguished of film buffs Barry Norman, awarded an honorary degree by the University of East Anglia and a frequent visitor to this region, can testify to the size of the debt the industry owes to a county hardly renowned for parting the curtains and revealing all to an adventure-seeking audience.

In compiling a list of the best 20 films projecting Norfolk as a centre of cultural excellence, I am sorry to omit such lavish musicals as Somerton Holiday, Oklaholkam and Singing in the Raynhams; tantalising costume dramas like The Pride and The Paston, Beau Guist and The Admirable Croxton; and wholesome Westerns in the mould of For a Few Ferrets More and Bad Day at North Creake. However, those deemed worthy of top billing are indeed exceptional in calibre and likely to collect bouquets in any roll of honour pieced together by film experts.

Here, then, the top 20 delights with a Norfolk tang, but in no particular order of merit.

> *Young Johnny announced with a smile,*
> *"I'll hev a hair-dew Punk Rocker style."*
> *Said his ma, "Dunt talk squit,*
> *Yew dew an' yew'll git*
> *A ding rown' the lug wi' my dwile!"*
>
> Margaret Loose (Blakeney)

- **One Flew Over The Turkey Shed** - Morality tale set largely in the skies over Great Witchingham just before the festive season. A plump creature destined for the dinner plate plots a dramatic escape, only to have the stuffing knocked out of all the scheming by a self-seeking bantam. Sheer gobbledegook - but fowl play suspected.

- **Diss Family Robinson** - Traditional fare. Family build a new home and a new life in inhospitable border country as they wait for the railway to bring prosperity. The Robinsons catch the gravy train, but it goes too fast for comfort. Telling flourish at the end as they pitch their tent on the banks of the Waveney.

- **Hingham High** - The first spaghetti Eastern. A brooding stranger, claiming to be the reincarnation of Abraham Lincoln, rides into town for fresh provisions, only to discover it is early-closing day. He exacts revenge at a nearby supermarket by refusing to buy cactus on special offer. He avoids a lynch mob at the checkout counter and stays to become sheriff.

- **Citizen Cane** - Epic story of a man with the fantastic idea of growing sugar on plantations at Limpenhoe and Lingwood and then processing it in a factory on the banks of the Yare at Cantley. He becomes a powerful newspaper tycoon instead when no-one will take the trouble to publish his adventures. Full of originality and invention, although it is a bizarre stretch of the imagination to call the factory foreman "Rosebud".

- **Carrowsell** - Spectacular musical with songs as hot as mustard! Flashback sequences particularly memorable as old Jeremiah Colman, benevolent mill-owner, starts a school for children of his employees. "Father of my People" and "Look what's left on the plate!" most hummable of many showstoppers.

- **Cocklestall Heroes** - Defiant fishermen stand up to the mighty bureaucrats of Brussels and a hostile European press who dub them "The Shellfish Shockers". Wonderful scenes as the EEC "pirates" try to board the fishing boats by leaping off Cromer Pier, hounded in their efforts by the angry cast of the summer show. In the Ealing mould, but for home consumption only.

- **Dr Acle and Mr Heydon** - Whimsical treatment of the eternal battle between Good and Evil. A retired estate agent moves to a quiet corner of the countryside. His long-lost brother, an unscrupulous property developer, seeks permission to build over 200 houses at the bottom of the garden of this rural retreat. The brothers never meet…

- **The Matlaske Falcon** - Private eye Sam Shovel digs up fresh clues in this novel treatment of the Dashiell Hammett crime melodrama. An archaeological dig unearths a priceless statuette and unleashes a trail of havoc across several villages. The L.A. background is more Lower Aylsham than Los Angeles, and this private eye is one of very few to accuse a suspect of talking "a load of old squit".

> *Billy got a job painting the yellow lines on the road. On the first day he covered 100 yards. On the second day he managed 50 yards. On the third day he was down to 10 yards.*
> *"What's the matter? Why are you doing less every day?" asked the foreman.*
> *"Well" said Billy, "The paint pot's gittin' further away".*

- **The Hound of the Basketmeals** - Black Shuck, whose eerie presence has hounded the Norfolk coast for hundreds of years, finds a modern setting. He terrorises holiday pubs where customers are used to having food with their drinks. Strangely, he ignores the old-fashioned hostelries where a half of mild lasts all evening…Slightly fanciful finale in the grand ring at Crufts, but enough authentic bits to satisfy Conan Doyle fans.

- **Cley Noon** - Classic confrontation between the hard-boiled native and the second-home stranger. The showdown over a plate of winkles in a birdwatchers' hide remains one of the most compelling in modern cinema. Haunting musical score and plenty of romantic interest as the locals plan big families in an effort to outnumber the incomers.

- **Coypu Eccles** - Norfolk's stirring answer to Crocodile Dundee - and note the neat cake connection! Our great white hunter leads the campaign to eradicate the area's most destructive pest. And when he's finished with speeding boats on the Broads, he turns to the coypu. Of course, being successful makes him another statistic on the jobless front, but he's ready for fresh challenges. Stand by for Grey Squirrel Nutloaf next year.

> *George was busy in his front garden when Joe walked past.*
> *"I're jest binter have a look at that Spring show down the willuj hall".*
> *"Oh, an' what dew they charge ter go in there these days?" asked George.*
> *"Well, I dunt rightly know cors I dint pay", Joe told him.*
> *"How'd yew manage that, bor?" George wanted to know.*
> *Joe told him, "I walked in backards an' they thowt I wus a' cummin owt".*

- **Paint Your Honeycart** - Voted "Best Musical Before Going on the Mains", it enjoyed record runs in the old Forehoe and Henstead and Mitford and Launditch Rural District Council areas. The film is mostly set during the Californian Gold Rush before it spilled over into Hemsby and Winterton. It relies less on plot than outstanding numbers like "I Was Born Under a Gooseberry Bush". When it first hit the screens, patrons were asked to bring ten small squares of newspaper to the cinema to hang on a nail on the adjoining seat.

- **The Canary Has Landed** - The one Jack Higgins forgot to write! This ripping yarn features enemy aliens from Suffolk infiltrating a Norfolk village in the hope of kidnapping Norwich City's star striker just days before the F.A. Cup Final at Wembley. Rather silly plot, as the Canaries were knocked out in round four. Cheerful romp for all that, and Ipswich Town go on to lift the trophy.

- **Caisterblanca** - You must remember this…an affectionate salute to the changing face of the seaside scene as time goes by. Marvellous final scene where an old fisherman casts his nets - and his soul - into an unknown future and picks up a creature at the bottom of his boat, "The Boy John".

He smiles as the sun sets and the water laps at his feet: "Here's looking at you, squid!".

- **The Godwickfather** - Heartfelt nod towards the Norfolk Rafia, a group of cottage industry pioneers near Tittleshall. Inspired in part by "Silas Marner", the main character Matt Table is wrongly accused of stealing ideas from a rival community the other side of Fakenham. A looms showdown…

- **Yaxham Doodle Dandy** - Oscar-laden musical with deft patriotic backdrops. A chicken farmer goes into vaudeville and waves the flag for free-range eggs. Rather unpromising material stitched together in thrilling fashion as our buskin-clad hero struts magnetically across the rural stage.

- **Ice Cold in Alby** - Family adventure set in the harsh winter of 1947. As the snow piles up, and the cupboards get barer, men and boys from two small villages battle across fields to get to the bakery for life-saving stocks. The bread becomes the obvious central symbol for wholesome country life, but the story is beautifully shot in black and white. Mostly white.

- **Scroby Dick** - Disney magic with a Norfolk flavour. A friendly white whale takes up residence just off Great Yarmouth and soon proves to be a big tourist attraction. He calls to the creatures in "The Kingdom of the Sea" on the Golden Mile to rebel and return to the wild. They demand half of the summer season's takings instead. Delightful satire on the holiday trade.

- **North by North Walsham** - The only film Alfred Hitchcock considered worthy of a Norfolk setting. A computer salesman from Thetford is mistaken for a spy, and enemy agents left over from "The Canary Has Landed" try to kill him. Chase sequence along the Southern Bypass is exciting, but the real drama unfolds when the salesman is run to ground by a crop-spraying tandem. Difficult to work out which side most of the characters are on, although Trunch W.I.'s rendition of "Jerusalem" puts them beyond the pale.

- **The Fransham Connection** - Cold War thriller in which all the players wear enigmatic smiles and knitted gloves. The "enemy" put a tail on everyone except the chap who has the Watercress File. Beautiful double-agents are either "Sinkers" or "Swimmers", according to their prowess in making good Norfolk dumplings, but they all end up in a right old stew. Rather dated, but the credits coming out of a bicycle pump still draw gasps of appreciation.

Norfolk Firsts

No. 8

Norfolk's first wind-up gramophone was pieced together by retired milkmaid Polly Marner at Horningtoft in 1878. She used a cartwheel, flute and foot pedal - and is believed to have discovered the television interlude by mistake. Polly retired when vinyl records were invented, but became honorary consultant to the Brunswick label. She turned down an invitation to appear on "Desert Island Discs" because she didn't want to leave the village.

Bard to Worse

NOW, if Will Shakespeare had been a Norfolk lad... an intriguing flight of fancy after sizing up the works of one of the most outstanding figures in English literature.

Well, he might have been born in Stratton Strawless rather than Stratford-on-Avon, and he might have helped build The Grand playhouse on the banks of the Yare rather than The Globe on the edge of the Thames. And then he was bound to have written The Domestication of the Ferret rather than The Taming of the Shrew.

Let's go from Bard to worse and light up a few suggestions for titles he could so easily have selected had he written those wonderful plays in Norfolk. Match the local version with the genuine article - but no peeping through the curtains!

> *Said the dentist while doing a drillin'*
> *"There's a hole here as big as a shillin'."*
> *He filled it with gold.*
> *Now my value, I'm told,*
> *Is assessed every time he's a' fillin'.*
>
> Evelyn Blyth (Honingham)

1. Lotter Squit Bowt Beggar Orl.
2. Pedlar of Swaffham.
3. Horry and Florry.
4. Good Larf Fuller Mistearkes.
5. Hossman of Acle.
6. Happy Mawthers of Winfarthing.
7. Cupple of Rum Clyents From Cromer.
8. Bit Dark Over Will's Mother's.
9. Roll-up.
10. Dunnow Noffin Bowt Them Sentimeters.
11. Ent Ser Bad if Nowun Git Hat.
12. Boy Hinry, King Hinry, an' Wot Happened Afore and Arter Hinry.

Shakespeare's originals:
1. Much Ado About Nothing.
2. The Merchant of Venice.
3. Romeo and Juliet (or Anthony and Cleopatra, or Troilus and Cressida)

4. The Comedy of Errors.
5. Timon of Athens.
6. The Merry Wives of Windsor.
7. The Two Gentlemen of Verona.
8. The Tempest.
9. Hamlet.
10. Measure For Measure
11. All's Well That Ends Well.
12. The History Plays.

> *"Excuse me George" said the foreman, "But why are you carrying one plank of wood when everybody else is carrying two?" "Cors they're tew bloomin' learzy ter mearke tew trips."*

Now imagine some of your favourite quotations from Shakespeare being afforded the full Norfolk treatment...

- From Richard III: - "A dickey! A dickey! My kingdom for a dickey, ole partner!".
- From Hamlet: - "Blarst me, poor ole Yorrick! Wunner the best, he wuz, allus a good larf and full o' squit".
- From Julius Caesar: - "Hey, my ole bewties, just yew cop a lug this way fer a minnit. I hev cum ter stick poor ole Caesar six foot under, nut ter say wot a good ole boy he allus wuz!".
- From Macbeth: - "Cleer orf, yew blarsted dawg!" (Out, damned spot, out I say!).
- From Anthony and Cleopatra: - "Yew scratch my back, an' Iyll scratch yours!". (I will praise any man that will praise me)
- From Henry IV, part 2: - "Ent that a rummun how he think he kin still dew orl them there things wot he ewsed to, but he carnt cors he's past it?". (Is it not strange that desire should so many years outlive performance?).
- From Romeo and Juliet: - "Cheerio, ole bewty! That ryte upset me ter see yer go, but Iyll be bowt fast thing in th' mornin'!". (Good night, good night! Parting is such sweet sorrow that I shall say good night till it be morrow).
- From The Tempest: - "Yew dunt owe nobody noffin when yew're dead an' gone". (He that dies pays all debts).
- From Twelfth Night: - "Jist cors yew git on yar high hoss, that dunt meen we hatter cum in the stable wi' yer!". (Dost thou think, because thou art virtuous, there shall be no more cakes and ale?).

> *A Norfolk labourer was invited to take a well-earned rest after 75 years service on the same farm. The old man retorted: "Blarst me, if I'd ha' known that wont gorter be parmnent, I wont niver ha' taken the blessed job!"*

Norfolk Firsts

No. 9

Norfolk's first audition for the title role in a silent film version of "The Saint" was held at Thursford Crawfish public house in 1910. Hezekiah Templar (standing, extreme right) reached the last three in the regional finals at Harlow - but didn't quoit make it.

The Name Game

WHICH Norfolk villages mean "the pirate's enclosure" and "gadfly island"? Correct - Ashmanhaugh and Bawsey. Let's try a harder one. Which Norfolk resort was named after large black birds? Bonus mark if you said Cromer - derived from crawe and mere - crows pond.

Obviously, the traveller would have seen plenty of these birds in this part of Norfolk between a thousand and 1500 years ago, and the place-name game can provide a wealth of information. Our ancestors picked the names carefully to describe the people, wildlife or countryside where they were based.

True derivations have been sorted out expertly by James Rye in "A Popular Guide to Norfolk Place-Names", published by the Larks Press in 1991. Even so, it can be considerable fun coming up with your own suggestions.

Several of the following were sent to me by BBC Radio Norfolk's Dinnertime Show listeners after an invitation to let imagination run riot a few years back. Ever since I have regarded every signpost on my Norfolk travels as a juicy challenge.

First, the county itself. In the old days the people could be rather suspicious of strangers and, just occasionally, territorially minded. Newcomers from other parts of the country were warned not to head this way. "Why not?" they would ask. "What's wrong with the Iceni?" Back came the answer - "They gnaw folk", although some early scholars of language suggested it might have been "They ignore folk". Either way, the county became known as "Norfolk", and explains why it was sparsely populated for so long.

> *There was an old woman of Wymondham*
> *Who purchased some rabbits and tymondham.*
> *They were cooked quite enough*
> *But were covered in flough*
> *'Cos the foolish old girl hadn't skymondham.*

Another school of thought gaining support is that the county was so named in the days before hosepipe bans and drought warnings when water levels were extremely high - "Noah Folk".

Try these suggestions for size - and join in the fun as you travel round the county.

- **Ashill** - scene of Norfolk's most famous smoking concerts in the early part of this century before they transferred to Hackford.
- **Aylsham** - named after the first hypochondriac to be diagnosed locally in the National Health Service. He recuperated at Feltwell.
- **Barney** - a rustic Mardi Gras where tempers could flare, especially if the "Best-Dressed Mawkin" contest was won by an outsider.
- **Barton Bendish** - Uri Geller once had a holiday home in this small settlement, where you could find a sudden fork in the road.
- **Bawdeswell** - comes from the cry of residents who ran bed-and-breakfast establishments in Chaucer's time as pilgrims approached ... "Come ye and reste awhile - four groats wille afforde ye bord as well!"
- **Belton** - traditional call of Norfolk wife to husband dressing in haste. This followed a series of embarrassing incidents involving a mediaeval swineherd who took a short cut past the lady of the manor's summerhouse.
- **Bintree** - resulted from the old country custom of tying a dustbin to a sycamore tree on Midsummer's Eve to ward off evil spirits. Fell into disuse after complaints about scattered rubbish.
- **Bircham** - last outpost of corporal punishment in the county. The head of the village school came from Waxham, taking over from the notorious sisters whose cruel reign ended in 1865. They came from Frettenham and Lopham.
- **Brancaster** - before the enclosure of land in 1572, a miller at this coastal settlement "hurleth sifted huskes of Corne for pleesing the Harveste gods". The ritual ended when it snowed in August, 1569, but the bran caster is still remembered for his productive years.
- **Burnham Overy** - originally "Burnham All Overy", referring to the wicked practice of incinerating awkward Britons by Roman conquerors.
- **Burston** - home of the first pay-as-you-leave public convenience in the Diss area. The penny dropped elsewhere, including Puddledock and Riddlesworth.

> Grandma was telling off one of her grandsons.
> "Trubble wi' young 'uns terday is they hev tew much munny ter spend. We had ter work long an' hard when I wuz yung, an' there wunt no tyme fer skylarkin' abowt. Dew yew know what your granfarther was gittin' when he married me?"
> "No" said the youngster. "And I bet he dint neither!"

- **Carbrooke** - settlement strangely named after excuse for lateness proffered by Iceni taxi-driver to an angry Queen Boadicea.
- **Castle Acre** - Royal Dentist's local headquarters. Ordinary mortals took their chances at Pulham Market or Gasthorpe.
- **Corpusty** - in memory of much-loved local baker whose meat pies were famous for miles. Satisfied customers would lick their lips and exclaim: "Cor! pasty" ... and the name has been doing the rounds ever since.
- **Dereham** - regular complaint to butcher, especially during the reign of Elizabeth I. Usual reply, laced with Norfolk wit, was to "go yew an' join Will Shakespeare when he ask for a cheap side!"

> *The parson was talking to the small children at Sunday School. "Now, Bertie, do you know where little boys and girls go when they do bad things?" "Yis" replied Bertie, "Behind Farmer Brown's barn!"*

- **Diss** - originally one of a famous pair in south Norfolk. The other community, long since disappeared, was called Datt.
- **Ditchingham** - this village name derived from a social meeting place where former sweethearts met to divide any spoils they might have collected together. A shrewd local opened an ale-house where those parting company could enjoy a civilised farewell with background music. "The Last Dance Saloon" once rivalled Gretna Green in the popularity stakes.
- **Edgefield** - village with a cricket ground where batsmen had all the luck. There were no boundaries at Runhall, and batsmen had to buy a round if they made a duck at Daffy Green. (See W. G. Grease's "Norfolk Cricket Curiosities", published by Bindertwine Books, 1911).
- **Egmere** - famous for being described by a passing culinary expert as "not so much a hamlet - more a tasty omelette!"
- **Elsing** - rather fanciful notion that this parish was named after the famous Spanish tenor, although there is no record of his giving a concert in the village hall.
- **Fakenham** - birthplace of the county's most notorious forgers, the Picasso Brothers.
- **Felmingham** - location of the first BBC television wildlife crew to penetrate the more rural parts of Norfolk. "We were really looking for David Attleborough" said a spokesman.

- **Great Cressingham** - another connection with The Great Summer Game. This village was named after a compliment to Ingham Cricket Club's travelling tea ladies for their outstanding sandwiches.

- **Great Snoring** - possibly the birthplace of Rip Van Winkle, although there are bigger dormitories in the county.

- **Great Moulton** - so called after a 16th century tragedy in this turkey-rearing area when a freak storm resulted in the complete loss of feathers by the whole flock. Members of a local coven were blamed, with locals muttering: "They've been witching'em!".

- **Halvergate** - named by a Norwich City Football Club chairman, who, when asked what the crowd was like at Carrow Road that afternoon, replied: "Hell of a gate!".

> *It was time for the annual village school play and Ernie had been given a part. He was very excited and rushed home to tell his parents.*
> *"Yew will come an' see it, wunt yer?"*
> *"Corse we will" said mum.*
> *"What part hev yew got?" asked dad.*
> *"Oh, I play a man celebreartin' his 25th weddin' anivarsery".*
> *"Niver mynd, boy" said dad, "Praps yew'll git a speakin' part next year!"*

- **Hickling** - catcalls in a Broadland village, usually aimed at coracle users going too fast. (Not to be confused with "Hick - Lyng", the way in which a student from that village introduced himself on "University Challenge".)

- **Hockering** - predictably from "Hock a ring", a 19th century pawnshop on the outskirts of the village.

- **Holt** - used to be an army garrison town, taking its name from the traditional sentry's challenge during the Great Gresham Mutiny of 1827.

- **Howe** - was an Indian reservation near the coypu's happy hunting ground. Big Chief Little Plumstead led the braves.

- **Lessingham** - a delightful example of Norfolk whimsy. The village earned its name from a declaration made by tipsy carol singers.

- **Limpenhoe** - here was formed the first agricultural commune for injured workers just after the Napoleonic Wars. Main benefactor was the Rev. William Spooner, in whose honour the second commune was set up at Spooner Row.

- **Melton Constable** - long before it became the "Crewe of Norfolk" on the railway map, this was a notorious location for police passing-out parades in August.

- **Norton Subcourse** - in the early part of this century a certain Davy Jones joined the Navy and embarked on a series of lectures on undersea warfare. He failed the examination with the lowest possible mark and was dismissed from the service. He retired to Norfolk and settled in "Nought On Sub Course".

- **Old Buckenham** - the county's first Country and Western music centre with rodeo riding for the over 80's was set up here.

- **Paston** - a famous burial place where priests carried out their duties to the letter.

- **Poringland** - derived from its location at the heart of the East Anglian rain belt. Other heavy falls at Booton and the Raynhams.

- **Pulham St. Mary** - this name resulted from encouragement given to a local bell-ringer canonised in 1324 AD. She was a milkmaid for many years.

- **Reedham** - emerged at about the same time as Belton, inspired by an old-fashioned cry from spouse flinging bills across the breakfast table. The customary reply echoed the qualities of other villages, most notably Binham and Banham.

- **Repps** - Norfolk's first college for commercial travellers was built here. It became Repps-with-Bastwick after the bad fire of 1921 when a bedside lamp exploded.

- **Saxlingham Nethergate** - named after a memorable reply from a farmer asked by his workers what they should do with items collected from the barn… "Sacks? Sling 'em near the gate"!

- **Scole** - site of the earliest known educational establishment in the county, originally spelt Skool.

> *The farmer and his wife carried a milk churn into the Fakenham bank and took it up to the counter.*
> *"What with orl them barglaries abowt we thowt we'd better start a bank acownt" said the farmer, removing the lid to show the churn was full of coins. It took the cashier some time to count it all out. When she said how much there was the farmer looked alarmed.*
> *"That carn't be ryte" he said.*
> *"Thas bowt fifteen pownd tew short."*
> *Suddenly his wife went red. "Yew know what we're bin an' dun, dunt yer?" she said.*
> *"We're gone an' bort the wrong churn."*

- **Seething** - once inhabited by a tribe at loggerheads with everyone. They were sorted out by Big Chief Little Plumstead and his braves from Howe at the battle of Hot and Cold Running Water.
- **Shelfanger** - first do-it-yourself evening classed held here. Wood Dalling and Hindringham (a course in civil disobedience) also very popular.
- **Sloley** - quite simply, the settlement named in honour of the true Norfolk way of life.
- **Stoke Holy Cross** - in old days when trains used to stop at the village, the fireman on the steam engine was most annoyed at being ordered to stoke the boiler when he had been looking forward to a good rest. The guard went along the platform shouting to boarding and alighting passengers: "Hurry up everyone...stoker's wholly crorss!". This was eventually accepted as the name of the station, although slightly corrupted in later years.
- **Three Holes** - the impecunious village cricket club could afford only three stumps, later sold to provide a bat. The three holes remain to this day as a salute to pioneering sportsmen.
- **Trimingham** - named in honour of National Toenail Cutting Day. Not to be confused with Crimplesham and National Hairdressing Week or Clippesby and the Annual Hedgegrowers' Convention.
- **Tuttington** - people liable to make mistakes never settled here.
- **Wymondham** - derived from the old custom whereby residents greeted strangers in their own special way - punching them in the stomach. If they recovered they would head for Downham in the hope of more civilised treatment.

Three ancient pillars of the local community occupy the bench facing the street window in the snug of the village pub. The silence is broken by one greybeard:
"Marster Parslow's cows jest gone down the street."
Five more minutes of silence. Then his neighbour speaks:
"They wunt Parslow's cows. They wuz Marster Wilson's cows."
Another five minutes of silence. Then the third member of the party rises to his feet, finishes his beer, spits in the fire and turns to the door muttering:
"Tew much argewfying here fer me. I'm gorn hoom."

norfolk firsts

No. 10

Norfolk's first mobile laundrette was opened at Ringland in 1934. Women were encouraged to wash their dirty linen in public while enjoying a good mardle when "Odds and Suds" came their way. Colourful Nellie Droy was in charge, but she threw in the towel when mechanisation threatened and sold out to Fakenham Laundry in 1949. She came from a long line of washerwomen

What They Mean

NORFOLK natives have a justifiable reputation for being disarmingly honest when it suits them - and deceptively subtle if the occasion demands.

This latter quality usually comes to the fore in dealing with newcomers.

It remains a matter for considerable debate as to how long you have to wait to be fully accepted into Norfolk society - some claim the qualification period has been cut to ten years as a result of threats from the European Court of Human Rights - but the need for tolerance and understanding on both sides cannot be underlined too often.

With this in mind, the Norfolk Bridge-Building Society have issued guidelines for those moving into the county who are keen to ingratiate themselves with the indigenous population. Comments most used by locals, especially at parish council meetings, down the village pub or in the bus shelter, are accompanied by helpful hints as to what they really mean.

Copies of the leaflet "Towards Peaceful Co-existence - Howld Yer Row an' Lissun!" are available from all reputable estate agents, mobile libraries and football pool collectors. Here's a selection to inspire a new sense of trust between native and newcomer:

- *"Hent sin yew rownd these parts afore..."* Obviously, you are a complete outsider, and I am at a loss to understand how you managed to get through passport control. Don't let this smile fool you; I am a dedicated xenophobic, and I would tell you so if I could pronounce it.

- *"I'll hev a harf, thankyer werry much..."* I suppose you think we old peasants can be bribed very easily? Well, let me make it abundantly clear that we usually sting newcomers and strangers for a short or two. There'll be no pity on tap should you have the audacity to try to curry favour again.

- *"Thass fairly quiet rownd here..."* We have always done things our way, and woe betide

> *The teacher was attempting to encourage good grammar.*
> *"You should never say, 'I saw him do it..."*
> *"Yis" piped up Horry at the back..."Speshally if yew ent sure he dunnit!"*

the pushy beggar who tried to change that! If you can't stand the sound of silence - along with crowing cockerels, spluttering tractors, Ethel's BSA Bantam and the church bells going like the clappers - go back where you came from!

- *"Darts team are away..."* Make the most of the peace and quiet because it will be rudely shattered when our sporting heroes return. They'll be back just before closing time. They'll be well-oiled if they win or draw. They'll be well-oiled if they lose, and want six more rounds to drown their sorrows. And I shouldn't be sitting on Curly Lambert's stool if I were you.

> *While knockin' an' toppin' the beet,*
> *David said to young Amy,*
> *"You're sweet.*
> *Come on, give us a kiss."*
> *Now they share wedded bliss*
> *With a small sugar-lump they've called Pete.*

- *"My nearber married a gal from Lunnun way..."* You'll soon discover that we simply do not talk to village people who have broken the unwritten commandments. It's bad enough having to live among all these foreigners, but to let them take marriage vows in St Boadicea's-on-the-Sosh...! Those with metropolitan inclinations must suffer the consequences.

- *"Yis, a few new howses..."* This village has been completely ruined by over-development, insensitive outside forces imposing their unnatural designs on an unsuspecting parish with the acquiescence of district and county authorities. Now they're trying to give us street lighting and put us on the mains!

- *"We're still close ter the land..."* Ernie Trotter is the last survivor of a proud agricultural tradition - and he only takes his horse to help out with the harvest if the combine breaks down. Nearly everyone in the village used to work on the farm. Now half of them don't have a clue where milk and eggs come from.

- *"They've dun up Lilac Cottage..."* Have you ever seen anything so pretentious in your life! The plastic gnomes are fighting the concrete angels over who should live closest to the wagon-wheel gates. And who can blame them for wanting to get clear of that orange patio! Could someone break the rustic spell and tell them "Tomatoe's and Cucumber's For Sale" should not be sprouting apostrophes.

- *"Skool's still open..."* You would have thought an educational establishment catering for over 70 pupils in a growing village would be safe. But parents, teachers, governors, children and the local paper have been forced to launch six survival campaigns in the last decade. That's as well as raising funds for books, computers and slates for the roof. Next on the agenda - inside toilets.

- *"Parish cowncil's allus bizzy..."* They had to call out the police last month after the vote for more housing. It was alleged that some councillors born in the village had met secretly at The Frisky Ferret beforehand to talk tactics. Scuffles broke out when the parish council chairman, Sid "Secondhand" Sykes, a recent arrival from Fulham, gave his casting vote in favour of more development.

- *"Wikker's a rum boy..."* The Reverend Giles Plunkett is from the evangelical wing of the Church of England, and he's organised guitar lessons for the Golden Threads Club. They discuss herbal remedies and Third World agriculture after choir practice, and he gets them singing and clapping during the collection on Sunday mornings so they don't notice how much they are putting in.

- *"Football teems a'dewin' well..."* The village side have to be introduced to each other every week because there are so many outsiders joining. Player-coach Jimmy Diamond flies over from Holland. Sponsors "Dialadwile Floor Cleaners" have promised to finance a new stand at the Sugar Beet Field End if the boys win promotion and do well in the Primary Cup.

- *"We lyke new people ter muck in..."* They move in. They know the lot. They take over. We let them get on with it. And if they should lower themselves to come and ask for advice, we pretend not to know what they are talking about. It saves a lot of arguments.

- *"Spooz thass changin' a bit..."* The last time I bumped into someone I knew from the village was at a British Legion branch meeting in Fakenham last year. I even forget who I am myself sometimes because nobody shouts out my name when I'm biking down the street. We used to argue and fall out over nothing in the old days. That kept us going. You could make up over a pint and get ready for the next bit of aggravation. Now you can go a whole month buying your own beer...

> *Old Charlie took two dozen empty beer bottles back to the Pickled Ferret. He placed the bag on the counter.*
> *"Dead 'uns?" inquired the landlord.*
> *"Yis" says Charlie, "And I wuz with 'em when they wuz a'dyin'!"*

norfolk firsts

No. 11

Norfolk's first bid to put man into space met with only partial success. Chuck Armstrong, a smallholder from Syderstone, spent several months in special training on a home-made runway at Sculthorpe in 1901. Despite the headline "Chuck's Away!" in the local paper, he cancelled his mission after wearing out the soles of his reinforced hobnail boots. "One small step for Norfolk…"

Diss Delights

DISSMISSIVE

Since men are born to want to kiss
And nothing more induces bliss
Than blithe Diss misses kisses,
A man who sought a wife in Diss
Could hardly find his life amiss
With some Diss miss his Mrs.
But if so be he miss in Diss
Accomplishment of so much bliss
(Diss misses him dismissing),
His easy remedy is this;
To give Diss misses all a miss
And kiss a miss of Gissing.

Reginald T. Bellamy

DISSERTATION

To Diss a young man came to live,
And there a trade began;
And lived though happy all his life,
A Diss-appointed man.

Great country customers he had,
And they were well supplied;
Yet while from Diss they bought his goods,
They felt Diss-satisfied.

The townfolk all approved of him
As honest, kind and just;
Yet while they should have trusted him,
They showed him much Diss-trust.

His funeral to the cold grave came,
And people have averred
That when they laid him in the grave,
His corpse was Diss-interred.

Norfolk Firsts

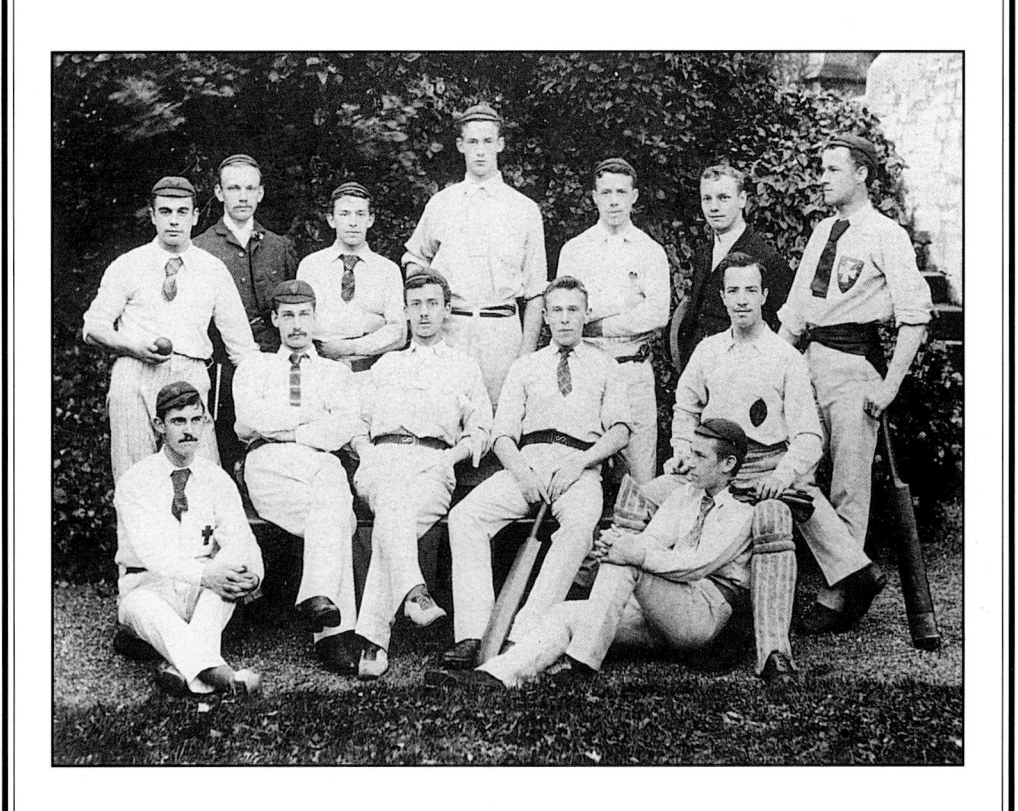

No. 12

Norfolk's first touring team of cricketers, the Rougham Ramblers, enjoyed an unbeaten run in Suffolk in the late summer of 1905. Opponents did not notice the Ramblers fielding 13 men in both games, although charabanc driver Sparky Spofforth and baggage manager Curly Moore did not trouble the scorers. They did trouble the young ladies of the locality at after-match celebrations.

Write Away!

I HAVE collected thousands of letters, many of them with a light-hearted flavour, since BBC Radio Norfolk started broadcasting in 1980. Listeners have relished all sorts of challenges, from the mysteries of belly-button fluff to memories of first day at school, often informing and enlightening me in their best joined-up writing. Here's just a small sample from the bulging files, the emphasis on Norfolk humour and the way some people can put it over.

• *Bob Burrows, of Weasenham*, showed how imagination can take flight...

During the war my father worked on a farm near King's Lynn when a German plane circled low after bombing Lynn Docks. The gunner fired a burst at him and an old lady in the farmyard. Thank goodness, both were missed. Well, when they filmed the Battle of Britain, they used three Heinkels over the Wash to simulate London. Dad was tractor-hoeing and heard the planes coming. He glanced up and saw crosses on the wings. He was off his seat and under the tractor before he remembered the war was over. Old habits die hard!

• *Doreen Hall, of Bradwell*, recalled how you can forget to be street-wise...

You've heard of people crashing their cars? Well, I managed to crash my pram. I was walking down Gorleston High Street pushing my pram with two small boys in it (one a few months old, the other two-and-a-half years) when I came across a group of women nattering in the middle of the pavement. As I approached, they kindly parted to let me through. What I didn't realise was that they were gathered round a post in the middle of the pavement. Prams in those days were rather taller than they are today, and I am not very big (5ft. 2in.). You've guessed it! When they split I couldn't see the post over the top of the pram. Bang! I pushed my pram straight into it.

> *"What a pretty little village!"* exclaimed the woman tourist to her husband. *"Let's go and ask that dear old chap over there all about it."*
> The old local was sitting in his usual place outside the pub. *"Would you be the oldest inhabitant?"* asked the woman. *"No"* replied the old man, *"He went and died last week."*

A bumpy ride for two small boys. A very red face for me.

• **Barbara Gedge, of Horstead,** sang husband Dick's praises…

His one and only experience as a member of a choir came when he was young and attending a small village school. They had entered a choir in a competition and reached the final to be held in Blackfriars Hall in Norwich. Dick was happy not to be included as he was unable to sing in tune. He was, and still is, the original groaner! However, as the final date approached several members were laid low by flu, and the rules of the competition stated the choir must consist of a certain number. To his utter dismay, Dick was given a few days to learn the words of the three songs, but he didn't attend the final practices. When the great day arrived Dick was threatened with all sorts of dire consequences if he actually sang. His job was to stand at the back and mime the words. He couldn't have made a bad job of it as the choir managed third prize. But Dick still wonders if he is the only chorister to take part in a competition - only to be forbidden to sing!

> *After much patience the village schoolmistress eventually found one pupil who knew that the word "trickled" meant to run slowly, and the word "anecdote" meant a short, funny tale.*
> *"Now, Horace" she said, "I want you to give us a sentence using both these words".*
> *"Please, Miss" said Horace cheerfully, "Our little dawg trickled down the street a' waggin' his anecdote!"*

• **Valerie Herrington, of Harleston,** chewed over the old days…

Many years ago, probably in the 1920s, one of my cousins, then about six years old, was staying with Grandma. Having no bathroom at that time, Grandma used to leave her false teeth in a little pot beside the sink each night. One morning as she put her teeth in, my cousin said, "Grandma, how ever do you get your teeth in?" She replied, "I just pop them in as you've just seen me do." She was quite amazed when the little chap replied: "Well, thass a rum 'un. I've been trying and trying - and I can't get 'em in!"

• **Aubrey Kerridge, of Wymondham,** put the accent on humour…

I've often heard you use the Norfolk word "mardle", and I thought you may like the following story regarding its use. Until I retired I was a police officer. About three years ago I was on patrol in Norwich city centre in full uniform. Outside Jarrolds, I met an ex-colleague and stopped for a chat. After a few minutes we were approached by a tourist who was obviously seeking directions. "I'm sorry to interrupt" she started off. "Oh, that's all right", I said, "We're only mardling." She looked surprised and then said: "Oh, I'm sorry. I thought you were a real policeman!" I think she'd been listening to too many "Mummerzet" Norfolk accents on TV.

> *The verger acted as a guide for a tour of the village church. He gave a detailed history of the building. One visitor was about to leave without so much as offering a tip or putting anything on the collection plate. As he reached the gate he heard the verger call out: "Scuse me, ole partner. If yew should fynd yew hent got yar wallet when yew git hoom, remember yew dint tearke it owt here."*

- ***Gwen Cooper, of Hempnall,*** proved the value of listening…

A few months ago we lost our beloved local undertaker, a true English gentleman and good friend to many. His business is now "under new management" with the full participation of his family, and is being run along the lines he would have wished and following the standards he maintained. Last Wednesday I travelled from Hempnall to Norwich on what we call "The Dinnertime Bus". On the way we picked up two ladies who sat just behind me. As we drove past the late undertaker's premises, the following conversation ensued:-

First Lady - "Ent that a shame to see that dear man's place so quiet these days?"

Second Lady - "Yis, that is. But I do hear that the chap woss taken over hev started up the funerals agin."

First Lady - "Oh, thass good. Now praps we shall see a bit more life about the place."

- ***Neville Day, also of Hempnall,*** also listened and remembered…

It was during Norwich City's famous F.A. Cup run of 1958-59. One Thursday morning after a replay I went to work and overheard two elderly cleaners talking:

"I see Norridge won agin larst night."

"Yeh, that wuz a good win anorl."

"Did yew lissun tew it on the wireless?"

"No, dint know that wuz on."

"Cors yew hatter hev a VHF ter git it."

"Well, I're got a GEC, an' I carnt git it."

- ***Ena Sturman, of Attleborough***, extracted this one from the past…

The dental story which always makes me smile took place in the late 1940s when I was a senior pupil at a girls' grammar school on the southern borders of the county. The school dentist had arrived to give everyone a check-up, the usual procedure before returning to give treatment to those issued with one of those dreaded forms. As seniors we were trusted to queue on our own and await our turn. Just ahead of me were identical twins. The elder twin's turn came and in she went. She returned a few moments later, smiling broadly and without a form. "Nothing to be done" she announced triumphantly. The younger twin said: "I'm scared." Without a word the elder sister changed cards, knocked and re-entered the dentist's room. We all waited with bated breath. The door opened - and I have never forgotten the look of horrified disgust on the elder twin's face as she came out, bearing one of the dreaded forms. She said in a hoarse whisper: "He says I've got to have one filled!"

• *Joan Hill, of Ashill,* had a brush with disaster…

It was during the last war - and the regular sweep had been called up. He left his brushes and other gear with the local handyman, "Happy" Robson. Our neighbours, whose kitchen chimney adjoined ours, wanted theirs swept. "Happy" came to do it and, of course, got the brush stuck. "No problem" he said. "I'll just go up on the roof and drop the ball and chain." My mother was baking bread, and had just put the dough to rise in front of the fire when there was an almighty clatter. Suddenly, the room was full of soot. Mother and I were speechless. "Happy" came to the back door, still smiling. He peered into the room and shouted to someone: "You were right…wrong chimney!", and disappeared. Seconds later he was back to ask: "Can I have my ball back, please?" This time, we were not speechless.

> *The rector based his morning sermon on the milk of human kindness and spoke at great length on local dairy farming to illustrate his theme. After the sermon, when he was shaking hands at the door, one old lady thanked him for his sermon about milk,*
> *"Mind yew" she added, "That'd bin a lot better if yew'd med it condensed!"*

• *Rachel Cooper, of Roughton,* was delighted when the penny dropped…

When taking the children to school over the last two years or so, I have passed a house named "Ribok" in Aylsham. I have always wondered what on earth it meant - till today when I noticed the full stops. Now I know it's a lovely bit of Norfolk humour…

"R.I.B.O.K."

• *Joyce Willcox, of Martham,* shared the facts of rural life…

Some years ago we took a niece of ours for a walk in the country. On returning she told her mother: "I saw some cows. They would have been bulls, but they'd been adopted."

• *John Tye, of Swanton Morley,* underlined the challenge of change…

A farmer was telling me about his first tractor. He sold his two horses and came home with a new tractor. He moved up to the straw stack, but couldn't remember how to stop. He kept shouting "Woo! Woo!" The tractor went into the stack and he couldn't get to the handle to start it. So he had to ask for his horses back to pull it out.

Norfolk Firsts

20839. A battered old salt

No. 13

Norfolk's first professional male model, Jules Jetty, known as "Chortler" to his closest friends. He specialised in oilskins and general seafaring wear, starring in countless fashion shows in the Morston area until he opened his own famous "Boateak" in Wells in 1911. Ganseys made out of samphire were not a success.

Bus Pass

COUNTRY buses have inspired many a good Norfolk yarn over the years. One of my favourites was brought to the laughter depot by Gerald Teeling, of Sedgeford, a prolific collector of tales with an earthy edge.

This true story comes from the late 1940s on the Fakenham to King's Lynn run. The bus concerned was a Bedford WD coach with straight cut gears, or crash gearboxes as they were known. The driver, well liked by all his passengers, was not very good at double declutching and so all his gear changes were noisy to say the least. He missed the trip one day, and a new and most capable driver was at the wheel.

A regular passenger, a lady who suffered from flatulence, boarded as usual at Burnham Deepdale. Before the bus had travelled very far she realised that her normal habit of relieving the pressure during gear changes was going to be difficult.

She hoped that when they turned from the main road at Holme for Ringstead and Sedgeford over the hills he would make some noise. No such luck. On to Fring, Shernborne and Sandringham. Still no noise, nowhere to take advantage. Through to Babingley and up to Castle Rising where the main road ran before the bypass was built.

By this time the dear lady was feeling desperate...But she knew the regular driver always made a terrible noise when they rounded the corner at the Black Horse. She prepared herself. When the driver's hand moved to the lever for that change to second gear - she let go. The wind roared through the bus. All conversation ceased.

To hide her embarrassment the woman said in a loud voice: "Driver, have you a timetable?"

"No, madam, I hent" he replied with no hint of a smirk. "But the next ole tree I pass, I'll grab yew a handful o' leaves."

Stanley got up to answer a knock at his door. A stranger stood there.

"Does Bertie Parker live here?"

"No, he dunt".

"Well, do you happen to know if he lives in this street?"

"Yis, he dew live in this street".

"Would you happen to know at what number?"

"No - but that'll be on the door".

Norfolk Firsts

No. 14

Norfolk's first "Roads to Prosperity" campaigners set out from the King's Head at Holt on October 12th, 1926. They are due to reach Westminster before long. Lack of dual carriageway out of the county has been blamed for relatively slow progress.

John Willy

MOTHER-IN-LAW has been on the receiving end of countless jokes and stories - but they dew diffrunt in Norfolk. I am grateful to Kathleen Hodds of Great Yarmouth for a couple of delightful yarns about her father-in-law, the colourful John Willy.

He was a builder, and always kept a set of sweep's brushes, needed when installing a new fireplace for a customer. One spring day his wife Alice stripped the living room ready for her big purge. She loved her spring-cleaning, always carried out between Easter and Whitsun - and always sheer hell for the rest of the family!

John Willy was given orders to bring the brushes home that night ready to sweep the chimney next morning. He did as he was told. Alice went to do her shopping next morning. When she arrived back the job was done. In the afternoon Alice cleaned up, emulsioned the ceiling and moved on next day to repainting the woodwork, polishing the furniture, shampooing the carpet and all the other jobs she loved to do. The family had to view the finished job.

The summer went by. Autumn came with colder evenings. A coal fire was lit. Picture the cosy domestic scene. Two dear old souls quietly watching television, she with her glass of Guinness, he with his slab of chocolate, sitting either side of the fireplace. Suddenly their quiet evening was turned into absolute chaos.

Without warning down the chimney came two or three lengths of cane and the brush. They flashed across the living room carpet, struck the French windows opposite. All hell broke loose as the furniture turned black.

John Willy tried to stay calm as he explained how he had simply forgotten the canes and brush had stuck. He was in the doghouse for several days.

The second ripping yarn features John Willy as an amateur dentist. His father, Old James Hodds, founder of the building firm in Manby Road at Yarmouth, lived next

> *Said the Queen ter har subjex, "My dares,*
> *I'm sure if you all sair yar prayers*
> *The sun'll breark trew!*
> *But I'm wass orf 'an yew,*
> *'Cors my reigner larsted fer years!"*
>
> Ivy West (Corpusty)

door to the workshop. When he retired, the old boy roamed round the place every day as he loved to watch the men carry out their duties.

One morning James complained that the only tooth he had left was playing up - this was the one that held his pipe in place - and he walked round the workshop holding his face day after day. Finally it was suggested he should visit a dentist.

Now, James did not part with his money too easily, and so his first retort came as no surprise: "How much is that gorn' ter corst me?" When he was told it would be about half-a-crown he snarled: "I arnt gorn' ter pay no dentist half-a-crown!" And he meant it.

Days dragged into weeks as his suffering continued. Now comes the gruesome operation at the end of one working day. The men packed away their tools. John Willy and James were still hovering. James was still muttering about his toothache. The ultimatum was issued: "Come yew on, father. I'll git that bludder ole tooth out for yew. Sit yew down on that sawin' stool." James did as he was bid, thinking, no doubt, of the money he would save. Two workmen were instructed to hold his head either side with others eagerly watching the operation.

"Now, sit yew still, father, this ent gorter hurt. I'll soon git that out fer yew. Thass a rotton ole stump ennyhow."

With the old man in position John Willy picked up a pair of pliers from the work bench, brushed away the sawdust and told the two lads to hold the head still.

He applied the tool to the offending tooth and had to twist and tug several times before it gave up the fight. James groaned and moaned as well as mustering some quite strong language to describe his son's heroic efforts.

The old man was presented with the tooth, placed with all due solemnity in the palm of his sweating hand. He sized up the rotten old molar for several moments as his audience chuckled. Then old James beamed: "That hev seft me a half-a-crown!"

He did a lap of honour round the neighbourhood showing how he had pulled a fast one over the dentist. John Willy went back to more orthodox pursuits in the workshop.

In the early days of motor cars, a rather posh vehicle conked out in the village of Filby. A crowd of local lads soon gathered. The driver, in goggles and all the smart leather gear, tinkered about for half-an-hour and then turned to one of the watching locals.
"I say, boy, just nip down the King's Head and try to get me some pliers."
The lad returned a few minutes later.
"Werry sorry, ole partner. They hent got no pliers ... so I bort yer twenty Gold Flearke insted."

norfolk firsts

No. 15

Norfolk's first talent competition winners, The Syncronised Seven of Saham Toney. Their highly original act, in which a ventriloquist's dummy made them all talk at once - but in different languages and without moving their lips - won top marks at a variety convention in Watton in May, 1874. The dummy, called Archie, had a Norfolk accent and went solo three years later.

Trendy List

NOW, your average Norfolk native is about as upwardly mobile as a sluggish schoolboy crawling round Grimes Graves.

A basic disregard for trends, manifest in golden moments like asking if a compact disc really makes the harrow more efficient. The least he can do is keep up with agricultural progress before diversification ploughs up more of the past.

However, while the Yuppy remains out of range, possibly still searching for the asparagus kettle in the back of the Golf, a new set of collective nouns is creeping on to the Norfolk stage.

I'm sure you can add to my list, culled from a pub snug notorious for its absence of *Yappies* (dog show regulars), *Yippees* (Country and Western fanatics) and *Tuppies* (people who wear you down at parties).

There's general condemnation of the *Thrummies*, the motor bike brigade revving up and down every village street, and the *Tooties*, your very own Dukes of Hazard with the musical horns they had for Christmas.

Once you've pushed a path through the *"Birmingham Navy"* on parade in Broadland, you can salute the *Yotties* and the *Yellerwellies*. Weekend visitors who chill the wine in case Fiona drops in for a spot of lobster. She can show her appreciation in several ways, all of them earning a chinless Chummywummy smile.

My favourites, however, are based firmly around any duckponds and thatched cottages left behind by the latest wagon train of local estate agents heading for the Home Counties.

They'll be back soon to add these outstanding characters to the brochures and the road show...

The parson was away on holiday and so the vicar from a nearby village came to take the Sunday morning service. After his sermon he apologised for it being on the short side.

"I did have a longer one all written out, but the dog got into the study and chewed up several of the pages."

As he was leaving, the old verger thanked him warmly for the service and whispered: "If ever that there dawg o' yours hev any pups, praps yew'll give one to owr parson..."

Yonders are rather aloof folk you talk about rather than talk to. A toss of the head indicates the distance between you and them. ***Yelpers*** are the settlers who start complaining ten years later that this isn't a patch on home. ***Yearners*** are the natives who wish the Yelpers would put that theory to the test - and take the Yonders with them.

Yawners have heard it all raging round them since time immoral. ***Yeasters*** pretend to work themselves into a ferment on behalf of all parties, join the parish council - and mellow into Yawners.

None of these should be confused with the ***Yarner***. He sits and fabricates in the pub snug, your average Norfolk native asked to reflect on the vagaries of lesser mortals.

Dora's Dumplins

Gal Dora med sum dumplins
As lyte as they could be
She popped 'em in a saucepan
An' say: "They'll do fer tea."

She poked the fire up fiercely
Ter meake 'em boil an' bubble
When suddenly the lid blew orff
An' started orl the trubble.

For them dumplins started bowncin'
To the ceilin' then the floor
Then they bownced ryte past har
An' way owt tru' the door.

Now Dora mearke har dumplins
The proper Norfolk way
But she'd never sin them bownce afore
Well, nut until terday!

Lil Landimore, East Dereham.

norfolk firsts

No. 16

Norfolk's first formation folk-dancing team, sponsored by the N.U.A.W., Stratton Strawless branch, Bob Hemp and the Bindertwines, were pitchforked into stardom with a cultural tour of Aylsham and district in the summer of 1907. They appeared regularly on radio in later years, most notably in "Educating Archie" and "Friday Night is Music Night".

Hello, my Bewty!

RAYMOND Chandler took the detective story from pulp magazines to a new level of style and acceptance. Philip Marlowe, undeniably Chandler's most durable creation, was making a rare trip to Norfolk.

The hard-boiled private eye would neither confirm nor deny strong rumours on the street that he wants to open an office in the county. He agreed to grant me an exclusive interview in a speakeasy not far from Pudding Norton.

Marlowe did admit there were nearly enough similarities between Norwich and his old home run in Los Angeles to tempt him beyond the occasional weekend visit.

"Still looking for Sunset Tower, Washington Boulevard and a few mansions, with wedding-cake decorations around double dormer windows and a Rolls-Royce Silver Wraith or Chrysler sedan living outside. But you're beginning to get the right idea" he smiled.

His clothes fitted him as though they had a soul of their own, not just a doubtful past. A broken halo of cigarette smoke sat over our table. There were heavy shadows under his eyes, a thick dark stubble on his broad chin.

He drank from the bottle, grimaced and fought off a burp, pushed the cork into the neck of the bottle and rammed it down with the heel of his hand.

"Liquor sharpens the memory. What was the question again?" Before I could pose it, he threw the answer somewhere towards the waitress with a mouth as red as a new fire-engine.

"I am 39 years old and have been for the last twenty years. I do not regard myself as a dead shot, but I can be pretty dangerous with a wet towel. I could be ready to invest a little bit of sentiment in this little old

> *The village roadman seemed to be having a bit of trouble when the vicar biked past. It looked as if the broom handle had come away from the head. On his return about two hours later the vicar was surprised to see the roadman still struggling. He got off his bike and asked what the difficulty might be. "Well, ole bewty, thass like this here" said the roadman. "I hev put the duzzy handle on twice…and now the head hev come orff!"*

Norfolk of yours. Then again, I could disappear as swiftly as I came."

I decided to test him out. "You're just another down-at-heel dick with romantic notions about easy pickings among simple country folk. You're just tired of the metropolitan muck-heap, the big-time racketeers and small-time crooks, the noise and stench of the interminable traffic, the emptiness and anger of hungry, sick, bored, desperate people…"

The look told me to shut up. "Got it in one, my little son of the soil." The smile was wide. About three-quarters of an inch. More drinks arrived in a couple of glasses you could have stood umbrellas in.

I tasted the ashes of the defeated, but kept on throwing the dice.

> *Old Charlie was receiving only nine shillings a week for working on the farm. The master approached him one morning and said: "I think you deserve a rise, Charlie. You can draw another shilling a week".*
> *"Thankyer, marster. I'll think it over".*
> *Next day Charlie went to the marster and said: "If thass all the same ter yew, dunt think I'll tearke that rise".*
> *"Why ever not Charlie? You put in a lot of hours here".*
> *Well, marster, thass like this here …If I miss harf a day, look how much more munny I'll hatter lose!"*

"But the only hoods you'll find round here keep the tractor drivers dry and warm…no-one buys you a drink - the Norfolk guy is so tight he squeaks when he takes his cap off…our skyscrapers hardly come up to your kneecaps…and our roads! Simply laughable, Mr Marlowe. Cart-tracks with raging acne would be a better description!"

He was revelling in my desperation, inhaling freely of that smell of fear he knew so well.

"Ideal for someone who has had it up to here with a career defying the probabilities, and marching just inside the borders of the possible." He threw up his hands like a naughty boy caught pilfering in the pantry.

"Okay, I borrowed that one from dear old John Buchan, and I'll take 39 extra steps to avoid it in future. But I am ready for a change, and I hear Norfolk is the honeypot with the lid coming off."

He lifted an imaginary lid as gently as an old maid stroking a cat, and tucked a toothpick a little farther back in the corner of his mouth.

I couldn't let my rising hatred boil over. I smiled, chuckled, guffawed, slapped my left thigh and choked all at once as the obvious crawled out of umbrella glass and smacked me between the eyes.

"No point in settling here, Mr Marlowe, no point at all! All those others, those pale imitations, they'd simply follow you here and steal all your business…!"

The blink and scowl gave way to a face long enough to wrap twice around his neck. I hit him with all I had before he could start untangling.

"Eliot Ness, Nero Wolfe, Ellery Queen, Sherlock Holmes, Maigret, Miss Marple, Hercule Poirot, Gideon of the Yard, Bergerac, Columbo, Charlie Chan, Inspector Clouseau, Perry Mason, Father Brown, Dixon of Dock Green, Dirty Harry, The Singing Detective…you open that door, Philip, my old son, and they'll follow like rats dancing behind the Pied Piper!"

Only the scowl was left. "I think you may be breathing, but it's a habit you're gonna break real soon, my little son of the soil. Take a running jump off that drawbridge and face facts. The true professionals are on the way, and you're too clueless to see it.

"Norfolk is ripe to be roused from The Big Sleep." Time for the showdown game.

"But that doesn't make me ready to say Farewell, My Lovely…" I was proud of that one. He nodded approval, but not so much as to disturb the ash on his cigarette.

"All right. Do it your way. You make it The Long Good-bye. But if you don't leave, I'll get somebody who will."

You don't form a debating society after advice like that. I got outside just in time to see a deep purple night ready to pick a fight with itself over Pudding Norton. Rain was falling, cold and steady, by the time I reached the pizza parlour.

The choices seemed to be multiplying by the hour, but neither food nor architecture were on my mind as she sauntered to my table and smiled a smile that had nothing to do with smiling. Mine wasn't much better. But I had words to go with it.

"Do you think the Department of the Environment sent him?"

Ephraim went to an evangelic meeting in a tent on the village common. The preacher ended his address with an eloquent description of the fire and brimstone and purgatory awaiting those who did not mend their ways, Then he spoke of the joy and bliss waiting in Heaven.
With a final flourish he shouted: "Now, my friends, stand up all who want to go to Heaven". Everyone stood up except Ephraim.
"What" said the preacher, "do you mean to say that you don't want to go to Heaven?"
"Well cors I dew" said Ephraim. "But not jist yit!"

norfolk firsts

No. 17

Norfolk's first do-it-yourself picture-framing studio was officially opened at Wood Rising in 1974 by a famous celebrity who surprised an invited audience by coming up through a trapdoor. "You can't see the join!" he exclaimed - but was told that was being wise after the event.

The Old Days

HE HADN'T seen the film. He hadn't been to the cinema since the war. But he liked the sound of the title.

"Back to the future" was a gospel he had preached many times to any of the village youngsters prepared to listen. Those occasions were becoming less frequent as his reputation for "going on and on about the old days" grew stronger.

But tolerance seemed to be in the air a few days before Christmas as he savoured his half and watched the office party building to a noisy but good-natured crescendo in the corner.

"Fancy another one before you risk getting breathalised on your bike?" The offer came over like a firm but friendly instruction. He slid his tankard gently towards the youth, who was affecting quite a balancing act with two trays and a dozen or so empty bottles and glasses.

Arthur was quite happy to be drawn into this early afternoon cosiness. He didn't recognise any of the young people, so perhaps they would appreciate a little bit of free advice as they stood on the threshold of adulthood and Christmas.

"This here back to the future lark you've been on about. I know it's a film on at the pictures, but that also sums up a lot of real life as well, you know."

The party fell quiet, and even two girls about to make a fresh choice on the jukebox postponed the pleasure to turn and join their friends looking at Arthur with a mixture of amusement and awe.

> *Gonzales Horner sat in the corner*
> *Pulling his Christmas crackers.*
> *One had gunpowder*
> *Which went off much louder*
> *And partially cracked his maraccas.*
>
> John Hammond (Beccles)

"I mean, you can't really work out where you're going less you know where you've been, and I reckon we ought to take more notice of the past if we want any sort of future worth talking about."

The youth who had replenished his tankard broke the silence.

"Eat your heart out, T. S. Eliot! Bit ambitious you thinking about a future, aint it pop? You'd be better off getting to grips with now instead of worrying about yesterday and tomorrow. Just be where it's at, and have another half. Try a short?"

One of the girls giggled over with a paper hat. She removed Arthur's cap, placed the flimsy purple crown in its place, teasing it into some sort of acceptable shape as it rested on his ears.

"There we are, pop." The youth was back with a whisky. "You are now a fully paid-up member of the Ambridge existentialist movement, living for the moment and any more good ones coming up between what is on the clock over there and chucking-out time."

Arthur took a tiny sip, young eyes concentrated on him as if the liquid possessed strange powers and was likely to change him from a harmless old rustic into a wild-eyed devil, snorting fire and abuse at a lost generation.

By the time he had swallowed his third short, most inhibitions and suspicions had gone. He chatted easily to the youngsters, accepting their guffaws of disbelief and modest nudges in the side as tokens of a blossoming friendship.

Arthur was the centre of attraction, and he loved it.

> *Two Norfolk labourers were hired to paint some flagpoles. One stood on the other's shoulders and reached up as far as he could. The foreman came by and wanted to know what they were doing.*
> *"We hev got to measure how high the pole is so we can work owt how much pearnt we're gorter need."*
> *"Dunt be ser sorft!" said the foreman. "Jest tearke the flagpole down an' lay it down on the grownd. Then yew kin measure it."*
> *"A bloomin' lot yew know, ole partner, we want ter find owt how high that is…not how long that myte be!"*

He told stories of his life on the land, embellishing countless dull days and back-breaking chores with little bursts of laughter and exaggerated portraits of colleagues long gone and places vastly changed.

He paused for breath and a swig at the end of the furrow, and then dwelt on the majesty and power of the horses that shared his agricultural load.

He summoned up a cavalcade of village characters who all knew each other, a community where you didn't have to advertise your troubles or your triumphs. They were obvious, and sympathy and celebration were automatic.

Misty-eyed now amid all the memories, Arthur felt the urge to go for the Christmas text. This was the time, the place.

"That's the sort of world we have to get back. Simple, maybe, but we could do with many of them there qualities today, and no mistake. Funny how people can be nice to each other at certain times, and then they get back to normal…"

He was in full torrent when the youth who specialised in missions to the bar put fingers to his lips as a signal for quiet. Arthur pulled up, suddenly aware of his own voice booming across the bar and bouncing back.

"We hear what you tell us, pop. We must learn from the past to understand the present and to enrich our future. Thanks for the advice, and thanks for your company. Time we were off. Happy Christmas, wise one of the fields!"

The party melted away. The jukebox was silent. Arthur's purple paper hat began to crumple and sag as his emotions fought to get out.

The barman began clearing the table, mopping up and tipping the contents of bulging ashtrays into a plastic bucket.

"Is that a tear in your eye, old partner? Everything okay?"

Arthur blinked and made a grab for his crown as it slid towards the all-purpose cloth sweeping across the table.

"Oh, I'm all right, ta. Nice to meet some really intelligent young people, that's all. They didn't mock an old man and his mardling. Just sorry I didn't get the chance to buy them a drink back."

The barman stopped his work and reached into his shirt pocket.

"Stop sniffling and wipe your eyes on this." He passed over a folded piece of paper.

"There we are - those lively young nephews and nieces of yours didn't want to deny you the pleasure. They could read your mind, so they've been putting all their drinks on your slate. Let's see, uncle…that's £27.77p. I'll settle for £27 cash."

> Old John was busy trimming his hedge when a stranger came up and asked how long it would take to walk into the village.
> "I carnt rightly say" said John. The stranger marched off in a huff. Then he heard John call him back.
> "Reckun that'll tearke yer bowt five minnits" he declared.
> "Well, why on earth could you not have told me that in the first place, my good man?" asked the stranger sharply.
> "Well, bor," explained John, "I dint know how farst yew wuz a' gorn ter walk then!"

Arthur betrayed nothing with his stare from beneath the crumpled purple crown. He did not move a muscle as the barman resumed his clearing-up operation.

"And a prosperous New Year, wise one of the fields!"

Faces pressed up against the pub window outside were soaked with tears of laughter. Arthur didn't see them, and he didn't hear them.

Norfolk firsts

No. 18

Norfolk's first ice-dance champions, Jean Norville and Christopher Bean from Skeyton. They won the county title in 1929 when the sea froze off Hunstanton while they were appearing in cabaret on the pier. Their novel way of getting back to the promenade in full costume brought them the first of many championships. Christopher Bean later went solo with a programme entitled "Freeze a Jolly Good Fellow". His former partner became a lollipop lady in Essex.

You Don't Say!

THERE are countless books crammed with quotable quotes on every subject under the sun…

- "It's a funny kind of month, October. For the really keen cricket fan it's when you realise that your wife left you in May" — *Denis Norden*.
- "Cauliflower is nothing but cabbage with a college education" — *Mark Twain*
- "I used to be Snow White, but I drifted" — *Mae West*
- "A diplomat is a man who always remembers a woman's birthday but never remembers her age" — *Robert Frost*
- "Ronald Reagan doesn't dye his hair - he's just prematurely orange" — *Gerald Ford*
- "I never hated a man enough to give him his diamonds back" — *Zsa Zsa Gabor*
- "There are three rules for writing a novel. Unfortunately, no-one knows what they are" — *Somerset Maugham*

Good examples of how to say something memorable for future generations to spread around the table at dinner parties. Add up the titters and admiring glances. Try to get through a whole evening without Oscar Wilde.

Then there's the Norfolk version inspired by Thoreau's message from 1854: "If a man does not keep pace with his companions, perhaps it is because

---

A young cricketer with public school experience moved to a new area and was picked to play in the big local derby against a neighbouring village. The game was away, and he made his own way there. He met a rustic leaning on the gate to the field of combat.

"Should be a close one, what?"

"Dunt reckon so atorl…weel marder yer".

"Jolly well see about that, my good fellow! Tell me, who scores most of your runs?"

"Marster Jenkins, the cowman's boy. Allus good fer fifty".

"And who, may I ask, takes most of your wickets?"

"Why… I dew".

"You? At your age? An opening bowler…?"

"Blarst me, no, bor…I'm the umpyre!"

he hears a different drummer. Let him step to the music which he hears, however measured or far away". Which really means dewin' different is a hoot. And they can't touch you for it.

I invited BBC Radio Norfolk listeners to join me on the march with a different drummer, beating a path to fresh areas of humour. The simple challenge was to get people to say things they wouldn't normally entertain in a thousand years. Here's the pick of the crop:

> *Billy was supposed to be thripence short of a shilling. He did odd jobs around the village. After he had finished chopping sticks for old Mrs. Burton she held out a fifty pence piece and a pound coin. "Take which you like" she told him.*
> *"Jimmy grabbed the pound coin. "Thankyer werry much. I'll tearke the littlest. My mum allus tell me nut ter be greedy."*

- "The Roman general is having tea with us at Quidenham" — *Queen Boadicea*
- "My feet are dry" – *King Canute*
- "I hate spiders" — *Robert the Bruce*
- "Prompt, please" — *Marcel Marceau*
- "Damn! I've broken <u>my</u> egg" — *housewife cooking breakfast*
- "I love it when people drop in unexpectedly" — *Greta Garbo*
- "I laughed and laughed until I got a stitch" — *Queen Victoria*
- "We're not going out in this weather" — *Henry Blogg, Cromer lifeboat coxswain*
- "One hundred and eighty!" — *William Tell*
- "If you don't stop following me I'll call a policeman" — *Pied Piper*
- "Come on, admit it, you've been seeing another man" — *Adam*
- "Wonder if I should dress for dinner" — *Tarzan*
- "I start work tomorrow" — *Andy Capp*
- "God Save The King" — *Oliver Cromwell*
- "Smart feller!" — *Dr. Spooner*
- "Oh, to be in England" — *Ronnie Biggs*
- "Get on your bike" — *car salesman*
- "What time is the tea break?" — *Florence Nightingale*
- "Give me a nice nut roast any day of the week" — *Bernard Matthews*
- "I've never lost anything in my life" — *Little Bo Peep*
- "Don't ask me, I haven't got a watch" — *policeman on the beat*
- "I think I'll call him Tuesday" — *Robinson Crusoe*
- "Is that the Isle of Wight over there?" — *Christopher Columbus*
- "Me and my husband" — *H.M. The Queen*
- "How much do I owe you?" — *Dick Turpin*
- "I think I'll get the bus" — *Will Kemp*

Norfolk Firsts

No. 19

Norfolk's first contestants in television's "It's A Knockout" were farming families from Bale, Heydon and Wheatacre. Here they are seen rehearsing for the "Find The Needle" game in the first round. Eddie Waring and Stuart Hall are feeding the elevators.

The Fame Game

WE'VE ALL done it with a smile bordering on a smirk. "You'll never guess who was sitting at the table in the corner - and I'm sure he winked at me".

Some reports are not so straightforward: "You know that girl who had an affair with the councillor's uncle in that programme they're repeating on Tuesday nights after the news? Well, her mother was at the check-out counter ..."

I recall nudging my wife as our honeymoon plane lifted off from Heathrow for Southern Ireland in August, 1983. "Look - there's Curtis Strange and Seve!" I couldn't say Severiano Ballesteros in those days, but I got in a fair bit of practice when he won the Irish Golf Open a few rounds later.

> *"How much are them melons?" Ben asked the greengrocer. "Seventy-five pence each or two for a pound" came the reply. "Right yew are then" said Ben. "Here's twenty-five pence, I'll hev the other one".*

My wife exacted a sort of revenge a few years back when her teatime greeting was spiced with the news that she was sure my favourite film star had passed her in a Cromer shop. She remains convinced James Stewart had come within touching distance. The Man from Laramie in Poppyland!

Brushes with the famous. You can dine out on them, and garnish fading tales with fresh titbits safe in the knowledge you are unlikely to be challenged by listeners anxious to share their own adventures.

Close encounters of the Royal kind may be common, especially in a county where the Royal Family are such regular visitors. But not all have been along orthodox lines. Tom Church, of Brumstead, outlined his big incident from August, 1940.

It was harvest time and Tom had been home for his dinner. At ten to one he set off back to work with his fourses bag on his back. As he pushed his bike he gave a customary glance towards the corner about thirty yards away to make sure nothing was coming. Tom saw a group of locals with a military policeman standing in front.

"He shouted something as I mounted my bike, but I thought they were just expecting some brass-hat. I'd only gone about a hundred yards down the road when I heard a roar behind me. Looking over my shoulder I saw four motor-bikes followed by two cars and then four more motor-bikes. They sounded their horns and I pulled in as close as possible to the side.

"They continued to hoot and this rather got my goat. How much room did they want? I was sorely tempted to give them what I would give any impatient road hog. I extended my right arm ... but at the very last second I changed my mind and gave a series of jerky thumbs-up instead. As the first car drew level I saw the Royal Standard, and sitting in the back was the uniformed King George VI.

"He was touring east coast defences. He briefly raised his hand as he passed and there was a ghost of a smile on his face as he spied my upturned thumb. All I got from the second car full of coppers was a frozen stare."

Tom thanked his lucky stars that he had changed his mind. "Had I given the salute I was tempted to give, I should most probably have ended up a guest in one of His Majesty's hotels!"

Derek Winner, of East Dereham, collected his claim to fame when he had a temporary job at the Royal Norfolk Show in the 1950s. He was put in charge of the part of the show ring that housed the show jumpers, and given strict orders not to let anyone in without a pass.

"A stroppy young lad tried to get in without a pass. I explained the situation. He said he was Harvey Smith, but that meant nothing to me. He didn't get in and so reported me to the show president. He told the young man I was simply doing as I had been told, and pointed out Master Smith would be the first to complain if their area was full of the general public.

"Master Smith must have thought I usually work in a pub as he mentioned something about a bar steward..."

Jan Adams, of Badingham in Suffolk, recalled how her husband also had a slightly painful brush with the famous. "He drove into a garage when there was none of this self-service squit. Leaning against the petrol pump was a really scruffy looking chap, and my husband said: 'Fill it up mate, please'. The rather petulant reply was: 'I'm Rod Stewart!' To which the old chap said 'I don't care what your name is…fill it up!' "

Malcolm Cook, of Toftwood, had a string of fascinating tales from his years in show business - like Bernard Bradon reversing his large American car into his Mini Cooper in Drury Lane. My favourite, however, concerned Malcolm's shopping trip to Marks and Spencer's in Oxford Street.

> *Little Martha came from the poorest family in the village. She went into the baker's shop and asked for a loaf of bread.*
> *"An' mum say will yew please cut it inter slices with a jammy knife".*

"A rather small and nasty lady gave me a hell of a telling-off. She said I should stop hanging around with that Terry now I was married. He was leading me astray and he should have stayed in the Army. This all mystified me until my wife saw the point - and explained that the little lady thought I was the actor Rodney Bewes and was referring to the Likely Lads!"

Of course, you never know who might be around when you fancy a drink. Bernie Blaseby, of Norwich, struck it rich twice while on holiday in California in 1984. He found an English-looking pub - a London double decker bus and a red telephone box were the subtle clues outside - and so he dropped in.

"I got into conversation with a charming lady, and it was only after about half-an-hour I realised I was in the company of film star Bette Davis. I went back to the same pub a week later and enjoyed a pint with Oliver Reed, who was off the hard stuff at the time. He taught me to play American bar skittles".

May Humphries, of Binham, knew Elton John when he was a young lad called Reg Dwight. She had a café just outside Watford. "He and his mates used to come in for coffee, and they called him 'Sunflower' because he hated going out in the rain".

May's mother worked with Terry Scott's mother in the Ever-Ready factory at Watford, and when May lived in Bushey, in Hertfordshire, her neighbour was the film star Shirley Eaton.

Eleanor Small, of East Dereham, passed on a tale from her grandfather that had been doing the rounds for many years. "A group of farm workers were working in the region of Sandringham when a party of Royal ladies came walking along. As Queen Alexandra was about to step along a narrow path, up steps one of the workers ... "Hold yew hard a minnit, Mum" he says, "Let's get them brumbles owter the way!"

> A customer at The Frisky Ferret looked out of the door of the bar and said: "Thass suffin dark outside".
> Billy took a look and swiftly replied: "That ent dark - I kin see Harbert's light"

Eleanor also related a "nearly" meeting. Whilst she was in the WAAF during the war, she was chosen to be one of the guard of honour when the King visited. But she sprained her ankle, and missed the big day.

Finally, one of those delightful round-the-houses stories from Joan Brown, of Langham. While her father-in-law was living in Canada he had to spend a considerable amount of time in hospital. Joan's husband - then only a small lad - was told on one of his visits that the gentleman in the bed next to father had shod Jesse James's horse on his last ride before getting shot. Now, that's real fame!

norfolk firsts

No. 20

Norfolk's first carvery was opened at Baconsthorpe by the Trotter Brothers in 1899. Nathaniel Trotter (left) became a vegetarian two years later, and the family firm was sold to a new grocery business in Sparham. Clarence Trotter (right) invested his share of the money in a new suit and became landlord of the Pig and Whistle pub at Swainsthorpe.

Dippy's Tune

DIPPY lived in a Norfolk village at the time when Norfolk villages could live quite happily with characters like Dippy.

He wasn't too bright, but there was no malice in suggestions from those who knew him best that he was "Thrippence short of a shilling" or had "a few slates missin' ".

Home was a caravan at the bottom of Jugglers' Meadow. He helped out on the farm at certain times of the year, and did odd jobs round the village in between.

Dippy whistled and smiled a lot, both pastimes blowing out his big red cheeks like balloons. His favourite tune was "Bye Bye Blackbird". He would stand on a stool for his party piece at the local pub, filling the bar with a mixture of laughter and admiration as he blew so hard and screwed up his eyes.

A Saturday night performance could bring him half-a-crown or more as the hat went round, as well as two or three halves of mild lined up on the bar. He could manage several pints before his head went funny, but he knew the landlord would tell him if he thought he'd had enough.

Dippy's impromptu concerts with bird impressions became more and more famous, and it was often standing room only as the curious from nearby villages joined the locals.

He insisted on two rules. Saturday night only, and just the one tune. It might last for up to ten minutes, but there was no encore, whatever the strength of the pleading or number of liquid inducements.

Widow Green was telling one of her friends how her recently departed husband always handed over his pay packet every week unopened.

"Oh, then I dunt reckun yew knew bowt that little job up Primrose Farm tew nights a week?"

"No, that I dint" growled the widow, and went straight round to the stonemason to get him to leave out the letters R.I.P. on the gravestone.

"Sorry, ole bewty. Thas tew learte ...thass already done".

"Right" said the widow, "Then will yew please add arter R.I.P. 'Till I come'."

> *Bertie was very fond of his pet canary. He let it out of the cage every day to spread its wings in a flight round the kitchen. One day it was frightened by the cat and flew up the chimney. When it came down it was heavily coated in soot. Bertie decided to wash the canary with the aid of a much-advertised soap powder.*
>
> *In walked Bertie's brother Fred, who was not convinced the soap powder would do the trick. In fact, he prophesied the bird would die. Next day Bertie told Fred the canary was dead. With much sarcasm Fred said he knew that would be the result. Harry put him right.*
>
> *"Blarst, no, bor. That wunt the soap powder what dunnit…that wuz the mangle!"*

Nor would Dippy listen to offers to take his talents on to other stages. He was happy on his own midden, still felt comfortable in front of all these people because most of them had come specially to hear him. He'd always been wary of crowds up to now, and that's why Saturday nights gave him so much pleasure.

The chest pains started just after his fried breakfast on the last Thursday before Christmas. Dippy felt bad enough to call at the farm house to ask if they would ring for a doctor. He was in hospital an hour later.

"Serious respiratory problems" was the bulletin passed round a subdued pub that night. More dramatic instincts took over by closing time with assertions that poor old Dippy was on his last legs. Yes, they'd miss him and his whistle …

The nurse banged the pillow as he bowed his head forward at her bidding. "You'll really enjoy the carols" she smiled. We've had some sheets done so you can follow the words. 'Hark The Herald' is my favourite. What's yours?"

Dippy's struggle of a reply was inaudible, although the chap in the bed next door tried to strike a helpful note.

"Looks like a 'Come All Ye Faithful' sort to me - and you can remain seated for verses two and three before we take up the collection!" The mild mimicry reminded the nurse she wouldn't get to church this Christmas. She'd have to put a bit extra into the singing tonight.

Trimmings above Dippy's bed trembled, and a couple of cards on his locker swayed dangerously as a draught ran along the ward to signal the entrance of the singers. Movement varied from bed to bed. A few patients could sit up straight. Most needed careful help to change position at all.

Dippy's eyes were closed as the carols began. He would wait until they were nearer before trying to raise his head. They were four or five carols away at least, although the accordion seemed much closer when it took over from the voices.

He was a child, feeling excitedly under the bed, cold and dark. Panic because there was nothing there. Guilt because there was nothing there. Guilt because he hadn't been to sleep. Morning was a black eternity away, but it dawned with its farmyard animals, puzzle and cracker.

He couldn't lose the child, warming himself on the first front-room fire since last Christmas and a family's smiles fashioned out of relief for a day away from the cold fields.

Boys with bigger presents and pretty sisters who would never look his way, not even when they let him carry the banner at the Sunday School parade. Now he was back in the classroom, teaching himself to believe the old adage: "Sticks and stones may break my bones, but nicknames will not hurt me".

"Dippy! Wake up, Dippy! You might have thought you'd come here for peace and quiet, throwing yourself on the tender mercies of the National Health Service for the duration of the Yuletide period. But we've got a surprise for you. Because tonight, Dippy, man of rural quality, village character extraordinaire and entertainer par excellence…this is your tune!"

A dozen or so smiling faces surrounded his white camp. A hand went up as if to admonish the accordion. It came down with an exaggerated flourish as lips were pursed and cheeks arranged for a Christmas concerto.

The ward was filled with whistling, nurses and patients joining in with the visitors to add "Bye Bye Blackbird" to the carol sheet. Dippy's eyes couldn't see for the tears, but he followed every note, recognised every voice as the pub entertainers wished him a happy Christmas.

They sang "It Came Upon A Midnight Clear" at the next bed. Dippy was fast asleep before they started the second verse, and he was carrying the lantern at the head of the line: "Pack up all my cares and woe, here I go, singing low…"

A holidaymaker and a local had been fishing on opposite banks of the river at Horning. They met in the local pub that evening. The holidaymaker greeted the local angler and said: "I caught a roach today and it was three feet long. How did you get on?"

The old Norfolk boy drained his glass, pushed it across the counter, smiled and scratched his head. "Dew you know I pulled out an ole lantern. Bowt a thousand years old, that wus. I'll tell yer suffin else. That was still alight".

The visitor was taken aback, because it was the done thing for the angler who had fared best to buy the next round. "What are we going to do about it?" he asked.

"Well, ole partner" replied the Norfolk sage, "If you tearke tew foot orf your roach. I'll blow the light owt in my lantern!"

Norfolk Firsts

No. 21

Norfolk's first meeting of Anglia Water shareholders was held, suitably enough, around the famous pump in Granny Bowden's garden in Poringland. The grand old lady of the village, in her 102nd year, invited the area manager to read out the latest share prices while the syndicate (including Splash the dog) looked on admiringly.

Dodman Lane

THE DRIFT presented the biggest challenge so far. So many ruts and puddles as well as disconcerting sounds of a dog agitating at the end of a chain a few hundred yards away.

Well over half of the singers wanted to turn round and resume their orthodox route towards the old council houses. Even if they struck it rich with a ten-bob note, it could hardly be worth all this effort.

More rain needled down as Ernie the leader and Mabel the musician walked on purposefully. Ernie's tilley lamp, on its annual outing, seemed to have a mind of its own, hissing and swinging on the end of a pole. Mabel's accordian was pulling her along. She went with a will.

"Not far now" encouraged Ernie, without even glancing behind to check on the latest mood of his Wednesday night troops. He knew all about traditional reluctance to make tracks down Dodman Lane.

Apart from the obvious hazards in winter, or whenever the weather turned sour, the lane had a reputation going back about thirty years. Well, it was more than a reputation; village history was etched with "true" stories about nasty fates and feelings befalling those who ventured along that pitted path.

Blackberry pickers, courting couples, Home Guard sorties during the war, daring schoolboys, delivery men from town - most missions bore testament to some kind of disturbing presence along Dodman Lane.

It was the boast of many a beer-filled Saturday night customer at the Wagon and Horses that he would defy the legendary forces of evil and "show 'em there ent noffin ter be frit of". But bluffs were called all too easily at turning-out time as a breeze sighed across the hedges and the moon played hide-and-seek with clouds and crooked branches.

Charlie and Fred were discussing their respective gardens over a pint at the village pub.
"Reckun thass a fine rose yew're got a' climbin' up fronter yar cottage. That fare ter cover every mite o' space" said Charlie.
"That dew" said Fred. "But I dunt hev noffin ter dew wi' that. I leave that ter the missus. She kin drive anything up the wall!"

Older villagers would mutter something about a murder at the turn of the century, but there was nothing specific in these allegations. Even so, the vaguest stories gather credence over the years if they have a juicy edge ...

Most of the blame for Dodman Lane's unhealthy reputation, still potent if hard to pull into focus, was pinned on the Nelson dynasty. The family had farmed at the bottom of the lane for at least five generations, and yarns about old Joshua Nelson's antics were still in circulation for a cheap laugh when darts matches at The Wagon and Horses needed spicing up.

There were no suggestions Andrew Nelson indulged in scandalous behaviour of any kind, although his personal cause might have been helped by the fact hardly anyone had seen him since he "came home" to the farm some five years before.

Surprise gave way to a spirit of bravado when Ernie the leader first suggested they should take the true spirit of Christmas down Dodman Lane. A journey into the unknown, perhaps, but this is the time to break down old barriers.

> Old Amos splashed out and took his wife to the pictures in Norwich. During the interval he went to get them an ice-cream each. In doing so he trod rather heavily on the toes of a posh lady further along the row. She scowled and muttered.
> On his return Amos was about to pass the same lady when he asked: "Excuse me, my bewty, did I tred on yar toes minnit or two back?"
> Expecting an apology the lady said with some indignation "Yes, you certainly did".
> "Oh, good" said Amos, "I hev got the right row arter all!"

Gradually, the singers had lost that sense of adventure despite Ernie's unflagging leadership and Mabel's brave support. Like youngsters drawing back from a musty old house, they tried to convince each other it was right to protest, quite proper to want to return to more familiar scenery.

Before the rebellion could break, they found themselves lined up for "As With Gladness Men Of Old," waiting for Mabel's starting note to punch a hole in the darkness, the uncertainty. Ernie's lamp was losing power. He had neglected pumping duty in favour of negotiating a careful route away from the restless dog.

He did his best to set a relaxed example, but it was impossible to disguise his own discomfort as they stumbled into the second verse. The carol dried up as Ernie and Mabel shuffled towards the door with collecting tin.

They returned several tentative taps and anxious glances later to a sullen huddle.

"Just a couple of verses of 'Hark The Herald', then we'll get back down the village for the last lap," said Ernie, forcing a smile and pumping fresh life into his tilley.

> *The vicar noticed that old Martha always bent her knee when either Christ or the Devil was mentioned. Asked about this apparently contradictory behaviour she said: "Well, bor, that dunt corst noffin ter be parlite …and yew never know…!"*

No power or conviction in either verse. Ernie and Mabel did tap a bit harder on the door this time, but again there was no response despite noises inside.

"Can't say we dint try…". They had scarcely rejoined the rest, ready for departure, when the whole yard lit up, a dazzling pin-table of orange and white blobs surrounding the village minstrels.

They shielded their eyes, shuddered with apprehension and then stood transfixed by the explosion of light ringing the farm world at the bottom of Dodman Lane.

At least three of them thought some terrible revenge was about to be wrought for all those Nelson stories they had either listened to in silence or repeated in idle gossip.

Another wondered coldly if it might not be the end of the world, for the whole bizarre business seemed to match many ingredients associated with Judgement Day sermons at chapel.

Mabel squeezed an involuntary scream from her accordian. Ernie was about to fall to his knees when a voice from above trumpeted across the cowering carollers…

"Welcome, my children, welcome. We have waited long for your message of peace and goodwill…"

The megaphoned voice dipped and lifted again as faces strained to see where it was coming from.

"We'll leave the Christmas lights on for your next item, if you would be so kind to continue your entertainment. And we Nelsons do promise not to spread any silly stories about Ernie and Mabel and others singing carols to the cowshed".

> *Young Johnny was caught red-handed scrumping apples in Farmer Wright's orchard.*
> *"Didn't you see my notice?" asked the irate farmer.*
> *"Cors I did" replied Johnny. "But that said 'Private', so I dint read enny more!"*

The gathering relaxed. giggled and accepted all the lights as friends. Christmas had come to the farm at the bottom of Dodman Lane.

Norfolk Firsts

No. 22

Norfolk's first sheltered housing scheme at Honingham was only a limited success. Lack of bathroom facilities at "Duntroshin" meant the male residents had to improvise at least once a week in warmer weather.

Rural Rides

I USED to find poetry of a sort in passing traffic. That was in my early blackberry-picking career, when jam-jars were just as familiar on the country roads as they were along the bountiful hedgerows.

We acknowledged a toot from every vehicle. A greeting as much as a warning. It broke the brambled spell as we turned with scratched knees and stained fingers to show we'd seen and heard.

It was most unusual not to recognise the driver as a car, van or tractor sauntered past, and we knew many of the number plates by heart. Here comes Ted from the village shop in his van - OPW 708. There goes the lady from the riding stables in her little Austin - ANG 522.

No points for the characters on bikes, although you could savour quite an illuminating mardle from the time an old boneshaker groaned into view until it disappeared through the hemlock and hogweed. "Mind how you go, old partner!"

Those spluttering jam-jars of blessed memory usually belonged to first-time buyers graduating carefully from learning sessions on the old aerodrome. We laughed as they struggled towards us, the driver peering and pinching the wheel - but it was affectionate laughter for a local trying to get on in the world.

> *There had been a hose-pipe ban and all the gardens in the village looked very parched. Except old John's garden. The man from the water board was rather suspicious so he called to remind John he could not use the mains water for his garden.*
> *"Dunt yew fret, bor" John told him. "Thass like this here - when we're got plenty we use it sparingly ... so when we hent got enny we're allus got some!"*

A motor-bike and sidecar combination signalled the appearance of him in goggles made for Biggles and her in billowing headscarf out of Nora Batty's wardrobe. As they sailed past our hedgerow hive, I often wondered if he was ever allowed out on his own.

A pony and trap, brisk and businesslike. A horse and cart, both the dealer and his cap set at a jaunty angle. The green bus collecting its human cargo around the villages for a day out in town or city.

An occasional cattle-float might make us hop over the dry ditch to the comparative safety of undergrowth battling with the barbed-wire. The first combine I remember emerged like a monster ready to eat up little boys as well as acres of corn up Red Barn Hill.

But in the main, country lane traffic wore a friendly smile.

Much of it stopped at regular intervals to prove that smile was genuine. The tradesmen trooped in like benevolent uncles. An ice-cream vendor with straw hat, a bike and a box brimming with inducements to good behaviour for at least five minutes. The postman who whistled in time with his pedalling. And such a variety of vans pulling up at the garden gate to remind us what day it was!

Ray Hooks with the bread; Gordon Bailey and Reggie Burleigh, grocery men with cardboard boxes we could keep for our shops; Lennie Sayer with the meat; the paraffin man; the Corona man; the accumulator man, who did magic at the back of the wireless so Dick Barton wouldn't keep disappearing. The coalman, who made jokes about getting the sack.

Even the Saturday dinnertime Indian with turban, bulging case and a delightful line in patter designed to soften the hearts of the most awkward Norfolk customers.

"Daddy very much like new tie!" - and out came a silk monstrosity with a nearly-nude lady cavorting across the kitchen table. Mother called it disgraceful. Father thought it slightly gaudy for the harvest festival services. The salesman searched in vain for more sober fare, and enjoyed his cup of tea before promising to speak Norfolk better on his next visit. "Goodness me, yes - I must get on same wavelength as Daddy!"

> *A romantic young girl from Old Catton,*
> *On her hols, fell in love with a Latin.*
> *She turned up at the church,*
> *But was left in the lurch,*
> *With a molto grand bulge in white satin.*
>
> Norman Guest (Norwich)

> *One of the election candidates noticed that Reuben had attended all the meetings in the village. On the eve of the poll he went to have a word and thank him for his support.*
> *"Well, bor, I hev been ter every meetin' fer orl four canderdates, an' I hev read orl yar leaflets an' pearpers."*
> *"Jolly good!" enthused the candidate.*
> *"And orl I kin say, ole partner, is thank heavens yew carnt orl git elected!"*

Jack Murton and Bruiser, the seemingly ageless newspaper men; Mr. Ulph, the immaculately-groomed insurance man who always had a kindly word for the children as he brought those important looking books up to date. His lessons in sound economic thinking might have been lost on me, but I have no trouble recalling his friendly manner.

Indeed, that is the main impression left behind by the whole cavalcade of country callers of my childhood. They were friends of the family, of the village, and that must have taken much of the sting out of parting with hard-earned money if that's what their visits ultimately entailed.

Of course, we used to hijack some of them with our plaintive pleas for a ride. Parents today would go cold at the thought of youngsters piling into the back of a bread van to embark on an expedition up a rutted drift to the farm on the other side of the world.

> *Several gifts were bestowed on the rector of a Norfolk village church as he moved on to pastures new. Among them, a bottle of choice cherries preserved in old brandy.*
> *The rector wrote a letter of thanks to the donor, saying how much he appreciated the handsome gift. He added: "But I appreciate even more the spirit in which they were sent!"*

Such trepidation is one indictment of the times in which we live. The fact that we did it, loved it and got back safely in time for dinner stands as a glowing tribute to the community spirit and trust that welded us together on the village rounds forty or so years ago.

There's much more traffic these days, but it races through, mocking memories and speed limits. One trip to the supermarket can fill the larder for three months. There aren't so many bountiful hedges, and you need to organise a search party to find blackberries free from chemical sprays.

> *A young Norfolk girl sought her grandfather's approval when she went on parade in a rather short outfit.*
> *"What dew yew think of my new dress?" she asked. Dunt yew think thas becoming?"*
> *The old man looked at her for a few moments. "Well, my bewty. That may be comin'… but when will that git here?"*

For all that, every plump and wholesome cluster demands to be part of our harvest festival as the mornings shake off the mists and the nights pull in.

A Sunday tea in winter in front of the fire asks for a jar of home-made jam. The passing traffic of childhood, and the tradesmen who stopped to chat and smile, won't be far away.

the last lullaby

No. 1

Norfolk's last great explorer, solo round-the-Broads Yachtsman "Scurvy" Skipper snatches forty winks after his oar-inspiring journey into the uncharted reedbeds of How Hill in "Coypew Hunter IV". He was awake in time to complete the perilous Hickling leg of his epic voyage before nightfall. "I aim to retire if I can get under Potter Heigham bridge and hear The Boy John's voice carried towards me on the evening breeze…"